TALKING ABOUT TOMORROW
a new radical politics

edited by
Stuart Wilks

PLUTO  PRESS
London•Boulder, Colorado

in association with **New Times**

This edition first published by
Pluto Press in association with *New Times*
345 Archway Road
London N6 5AA
and 5500 Central Avenue
Boulder, Colorado 80301, USA

Seeking a Radical Party first published in *New Times* 21, 17 Oct 1992
Reviving Socialism first published in *New Times* 20, 3 Oct 1992
New Directions for Labour first published in *New Times* 27, 23 Jan 1993
The Unions' New Agenda first published in *New Times* 33, 17 Apr 1993
Three-thirds Britain first published in *New Times* 35, 15 May 1993
What is Wrong with Britain's Economy? first published in *New Times* 32, 3 Apr 1993
Building a Green and More Sustainable Society first published in *New Times* 32, 3 Apr 1993
It Does Not Have to be Like This first published in *New Times* 32, 3 Apr 1993
Back to Beveridge first published in *New Times* 34, 1 May 1993
Social Justice first published in *New Times* 31, 20 Mar 1993
Poverty Demobilises first published in *New Times* 22, 31 Oct 1992
Strong Medicine first published in *New Times* 33, 17 Apr 1993
For a Radical Democracy first published in *New Times* 17, 8 Aug 1992
Embracing Equality and Difference first published in *New Times* 19, 19 Sept 1992
A Radical Left Project first published in *New Times* 18, 5 Sept 1992
Democracy by Instalments first published in *New Times* 36, 29 May 1993
The Party's Over first published in *New Times* 29, 20 Feb 1993
The Earth's Rocky Road from Rio first published in *New Times* 16, 25 July1992
Troubled Pleasure first published in *New Times* 23, 14 Nov 1992
Hite Strikes Back first published in *New Times* 30, 6 Mar 1993
Opening Up Our Vision first published in *New Times* 14, 27 Jun 1992

Collection © *New Times* 1993

British Library Cataloguing in Publication Data

A catalogue record for this book is available from the British Library

Library of Congress Cataloging in Publication data applied for

ISBN 0 7453 0792 2 hb
ISBN 0 7453 0793 0 pb

Produced for Pluto Press by Chase Production Services
Designed and typeset by *New Times*
Printed in Finland by WSOY

Contents

Notes on Contributors

Frank Blackaby is an economist and was formerly Director of the Stockholm International Peace Research Institute.

Sir Gordon Borrie is Chair of the Labour Party's Commission on Social Justice.

Beatrix Campbell is a journalist and broadcaster. Her most recent book *Goliath* was published in 1993.

Anne Coddington is deputy editor of *New Times*.

Kevin Davey is lecturer in Journalism at Hackney College and a former chair of the Socialist Society.

David Donnision is Professor of Town and Regional Planning at the University of Glasgow.

Nina Fishman lectures in History and Industrial Relations at the University of Westminster. Her book *The British Communist Party and the Trade Unions 1933-45*, is published by Scholar Press in 1993.

Quentin Given is an Environmental Health Officer for the London Borough of Camden.

Stuart Hall is professor of sociology at the Open University.

Shere Hite is a well known US feminist and author of *The Hite Report on Female Sexuality*. Her latest book *Women as Revolutionary Agents of Change* is published by Bloomsbury in 1993.

Will Hutton is economics editor for the *Guardian*.

Dr Steve Iliffe is a London G.P. and author of *Strong Medicine*.

Michael Jacobs is a consultant and writer on local economic development and environmental policy and author of *The Green Economy*.

William Keegan is economics editor of the *Observer*. His latest book *The Spectre of Capitalism* was published in 1992.

Ernesto Laclau is Professor of Sociology at the University of Essex.

Adam Lent is completing a Phd on the changes in the British Labour Party since 1983 at the University of Sheffield. He writes regularly for *New Times*.

David Marquand is Professor of Politics at the University of Sheffield.

Michael Meacher is Labour MP for Oldham West and is chief opposition spokesperson on Overseas Development and Cooperation. His book *Diffusing Power: The Key to Socialist Revival* was published in July 1992.

John Monks is General Secretary of the TUC.

Chantal Mouffe teaches at the Collège International de Philosophie in Paris where she is in charge of a programme on 'Citizenship and Modern Democracy'. Her next book, *The Return of the Political*, will be published by Verso in the autumn of 1993.

Geoff Mulgan is director of Demos, an independent think tank.

Jonathon Porritt is a former director of Friends of the Earth and author of *Seeing Green* and *The Coming of the Greens*.

Mike Power is the editor of *New Times*.

Mike Rustin is Professor of Sociology at the University of East London.

Denise Searle is launch editor of *Red Pepper* and formerly editor of *Socialist*.

Anne Showstack Sassoon is Professor in Politics at Kingston University. She is author of *Gramsci's Politics* and editor of *Women and the State*.

Kate Soper is a writer, translator and lecturer in Philosophy at the University of North London.

Noni Stacey is a financial journalist.

Nina Temple is Federal Secretary of Democratic Left and was formerly Secretary of the Communist Party of Great Britain.

Willie Thompson is Senior Lecturer in History at Glasgow Caledonian University and author of *The Good Old Cause: British Communism 1920-1991* and *The Long Death of British Labourism*.

Stuart Wilks is Lecturer in Urban Studies at the University of Humberside, Hull. He was formerly Senior Research Officer in the Institute of Management at the London School of Economics and is a regular contributor to *New Times*.

PREFACE

IT IS NOT by accident that this open ended, questioning and optimistic book should have been produced by Democratic Left's journal *New Times*. This is because Democratic Left, which has been described both as a grassroots think tank and a catalyst for change, is prepared to be positively uncertain rather than proscribing simple solutions to difficult problems and seeks new thinking through dialogue and difference.

The failure and final collapse of communism in 1989 fundamentally changed the political landscape and altered the nature of the challenges facing all those who want to see social justice. But these far reaching implications were denied by many from the labour and left traditions. They chose to portray communism as something alien and completely separate rather than to recognise the connections between communism and the wider left. However, the possibility of denying any such connection was clearly not available to members of the Communist Party in 1989, because even the most reform-minded members were linked symbolically by the name.

Through acknowledging the wider implications of the collapse of communism, the party's journal *Marxism Today* was able to recognise a moment of epochal change in an analysis which it called New Times. This analysis encompassed the collapse of the post-war settlement, globally and in Europe, with the end of the cold war, and in Britain with the exhaustion of labourism. It recognised the impact of the new post-Fordist industrial revolution driven by high-technology, and the growing environmental and developmental imperatives. It argued that such was the scale of change that previous socialist certainties became irrelevant. The Communist Party applied this analysis to itself. It recognised the historic failure of the bolshevik tradition in which it had itself been cast and the authoritarian nature of its organisational command structures. It therefore set about reinventing itself. The 43rd and final congress of the Communist Party in 1991 agreed to transform the party into Democratic Left.

In many ways Democratic Left is a cultural antithesis of its former self. It is based on values rather than ideology, it is open rather than closed, and federal and pluralist rather than monolithic; but it does aim to take forward the best of the British communist tradition. This tradition involved people in an active campaigning and intellectual politics; believing that ultimately the political agenda can be shaped by the 'caring, sharing and daring' of active citizens rather than being handed down from on high. Democratic Left held its first conference in June 1993 and set out a radical and experimental role for itself, existing in the space between parliamentary political parties and single issue pressure groups, but developing links with both. It is seeking to establish local forums for dialogue, to serve as a focus for campaigns, and be open to and promote radical democratic thinking. It has replaced all ideas of a vanguard role with the notion of enabling members to effectively develop their own interests, contributing to the creation of the far reaching coalitions that will be required to achieve a democratic, social and environmental renovation of our society.

Nina Temple
Federal Secretary, Democratic Left

INTRODUCTION

Stuart Wilks

THIS BOOK CONSISTS of a collection of interviews and articles, originally published in *New Times*, the journal of Democratic Left and now substantially rewritten and updated. It is a book which urges the left to look forward. Unfortunately, 'look forward' is not meant here in the optimistic sense of knowing that something pleasantly progressive is just around the corner, but as a statement of intent; a counterbalance to the understandable temptation to project doom and gloom on the left. However, the fact remains that any search for new roads to left revival must necessarily begin from a stark recognition of the realities for the left in the late twentieth century – that it faces a deep and profound crisis. In short, we are not talking about tomorrow just because we cannot face talking about today.

The left's inability to look forward is not, as is often suggested, merely a problem of vision. Unfortunate, because compared to other deficiencies, vision is relatively easy to correct. Our crisis is more profound; it is a multidimensional malaise. On every imaginable level the left is in rapid decline. In the popular mind, the politics of the left, the politics of 'socialism' and 'communism', is a failed politics, with little or no relevance to the world as we approach the next millennium. Among the intellectuals, the search for new alternatives has reached a spectacularly sparse plateau of thought. Radical views are being silenced ever more rapidly, by a means far more potent than the machinery of state censorship – by the market mechanism, which pronounces that the demand for radical publications is quickly diminishing. And the Labour Party, overwhelmingly the most important and influential institution of the left, becomes ever more mainstream, and yet seems evermore unable to win a General Election. This is a crisis of thinking, a crisis of support, a crisis of resources but perhaps above all else a crisis of courage – the left is burying its head in the sands of history rather than recognising the painful realities of the present. Perhaps most worrying of all for the left is a point often lost among the factionalism of its politics – that because the malaise is multifaceted, the crisis of the whole is, undoubtably, greater than the sum of the crises of the parts.

This critical juncture requires us to think seriously about our role. If there is to be a revival of the left, we must engage in an exchange of ideas: a difficult and, in all likelihood, painful exchange. But it is an exchange which must take place if we are to build the alliances which will be pivotal to any future left strategy. As the title of this book suggests, it is time to talk about tomorrow. But we must do so with an understanding of the mistakes of the past and of the realities of the present.

Talking about Tomorrow is a bold first step in opening up this exchange and forging new left alliances. It is an exercise that will no doubt be subject to mocking criticism by some on the left who will ask, quite rightly – how is talking going to help? These cynics will say that there is one simple answer – 'less talk and more action' and a return to good old-fashioned class struggle. This is a critical point of departure. One of the central contentions of this book is that a return to the old-fashioned politics of the left is a return to a stage of history which has long since passed. If we are to stop the rot, the left must start to transform itself by facing the future, via the realities of the present. But there are things in history which the left needs to return to and in this sense the left does not so much need to transform itself for the future as *return* to a process of transforming itself which began in its not too distant past.

The process of left transformation began some quarter of a century ago with the rise of the new left in the 1960s, a reminder that the so called 'new politics' is perhaps older than is commonly thought. However, the transformation never came to fruition; there was only a partial change in the nature of left politics and the necessary shift from the politics of the old to the politics of the new has failed to materialise. The source of the left's sorrows is that in the course of the last part of the twentieth century we have trapped ourselves. We have trapped ourselves between two agendas – that of the old left and that of the new politics.

In western Europe, the dominant politics of the old left

emerged in the mid twentieth century as the politics of social democratic reformism. The politics, and the considerable strength, of the old left was typified by the Keynesian welfare state, an essentially social democratic compromise which accepted the virtues of a mixed economy managed by the government in concert with unions and employers, using Keynesian techniques to guarantee full employment and economic growth which became the essential foundations for the establishment and growth of the welfare state. In essence, the so called post-war consensus was actually about settling the debates of the 1930s. Hence, in Britain, the Labour government of 1945-51 introduced the policies and institutions which embodied a consensus which had emerged during the war years but which had been the focus of fierce debate 15 years before.

Two decades were to pass before the consensus came under any serious strain and, as is now often forgotten, it first came under strain from the left. The emergence of radical feminist and environmentalist perspectives in the 1960s challenged the old politics of the left – the class-based politics of 'labourism'. The rise of the new left was inspired by a recognition that the socialist project, in all its variants, from social democratic reformism to communist totalitarianism, had become narrowly statist in orientation. To the new left, socialism had become stifling, anti-individualist and monolithic.

The new left critique of these statist solutions was the beginning of the vital transformation of the left. However, it was a transformation which was to be halted in its tracks, principally because the left was outmanoeuvred by the right. The individualist agenda, which had been squeezed out by the collectivism of the socialist project, was picked up by the right in their transition from paternalism to radicalism. With the emergence of the new right came a powerful, and initially popular, attack on the institutional and policy foundations of the post-war consensus. The new right offensive threw the left back into defence of the institutions it had only just begun to reassess. Partly out of necessity, the left has continued to adopt this position of defence. But it has been a damaging defence, not only because so many battles have been lost along the way but also because it has meant that the new agenda of the left has never been able to mature.

The critical questions for the left in the late twentieth century relate to its position between the old and new agendas. Which parts of the old agenda should we seek to defend and to revive? And how? Or should we be looking to advance an entirely new agenda for the twenty-first century? With the ruins of the post-war consensus around us, we must ask how much of it, if any, we will seek to rebuild? Should our focus be a case for full employment and the welfare state or on individual empowerment and a far reaching democratisation of society? Should we seek to use the state to achieve social justice or should we be looking to break up the state and diffuse power? Can left politics continue to be class-based or is it time to recognise that the only prospect for progressive politics is to start on the difficult task of building coalitions across what may be deeper cleavages than socio-economic groups – those of gender, race and age?

The transition from the old politics of the left to a new radicalism will not be easy. For one, the strength of the old politics, the powerful politics of labourism, was built on a solidarity emanating from the common experiences of exploitation among the male working majority of industrial capitalism. The factory system forged a powerful class consciousness which made mass mobilisation both possible and potent. And in the mid twentieth century the Keynesian welfare state emerged as the embodiment of a class compromise marking the zenith of the power of labour to challenge capital.

But the class base of labourism has long been undermined and whatever the claims that in a 'two-thirds one-third' society as Britain is today, class divisions are as prevalent as ever, the essential point remains that the class-based support of the old socialism no longer exists. Moreover, class structures have changed because capitalism has changed and the new economic base is one which Marx could never have imagined. Usually described as a transition from Fordist to post-Fordist production (a shift from centralised mass production to market diversification and decentralised organisational structures) the new form of industrial capitalism in the developed world has, in consequence, helped to bring about the apparent demise of the Keynesian full employment policies designed for Fordist economic structures. The demise of Keynesianism, a key element of the social democratic consensus, in turn, has come to threaten the basis of the universalist welfare state.

Recognition of the changing nature of capitalism and of the

social structures which it produces was a major part of the contribution of *Marxism Today* to British political debate in the 1970s and 1980s. In this period, the Communist Party of Great Britain became the main force on the left arguing for a new conception of socialism. Finally, in January 1992, after years of financial difficulty, *Marxism Today* ran its final edition as the Communist Party, which had subsidised the highly influential journal for almost 35 years, was wound up and reconstituted as Democratic Left.

In a cold climate for socialism, Democratic Left has sought to draw on creative Marxism, feminism and environmentalism to construct a vision of left politics which is democratic, pluralistic and sustainable. As part of this wider political project, the party's journal, *New Times*, named after *Marxism Today*'s celebrated characterisation of modern politics and economics, has continued where *Marxism Today* left off – with the difficult task of helping to understand the nature and forge the identity of the new politics.

This collection of interviews and articles represents part of this search for the foundations of a challenging new left alternative. The contributors to this book are assessing what remains of the social democratic project and of the labour movement which sustained it. The discussions which follow are also trying to pin down the elusive new politics and the nature of the new left project.

The starting point for any discussion of the left in Britain today must be the Labour Party and the trade unions, if only because labourism has, historically, been the most significant force and ideology of the left. Section one of this book therefore examines the current state of the labour movement and the Labour Party from the perspective of the radical left.

In the first interview, David Marquand's discussion with Nina Fishman draws out the historical context of the British socialist tradition. Marquand argues that the Labour Party became assimilated into a form of 'bankrupt Whiggery' which broke down in the 1970s. For Marquand, the critical failure of Labour was to accept, unequivocally, the use of state power as a means to pursue its policies rather than seeking to restructure the institutions of a bankrupt state left largely unchanged by the events of 1848. By accepting rather than challenging Britain's archaic political institutions, Labour shows little sign of being the radical party Marquand hopes for. Yet, he confesses, there appears to be no real alternative.

Labour MP Michael Meacher, however, believes that the Labour Party and socialism can be revived through a radical policy of diffusing state power. Talking to *New Times* editor, Mike Power, Meacher defends his 'great affection for the socialist idea' against claims that he is approaching socialism from a discredited and disliked statist conception. Meacher's defence is that socialism retains its relevance while power, both political and economic, remains centralised and concentrated in relatively few hands. To win a parliamentary majority under first-past-the-post, an electoral system which Meacher does not seriously question, Labour must develop a new vision of social justice and diffused state power rather than appearing 'ultra respectable' and going 'to the city for swish dinners' with the people they 'really intend to take on'.

A key theme running through the first set of interviews is the position of class politics in a post-Fordist economy. *Marxism Today's* analysis in the 1980s had provoked sharp criticism from, among others, Mike Rustin, whose interview with Kevin Davey is the next in this section. Here Rustin argues that one danger implicit in the New Times argument is that it obscures the true nature of the change which, at root, is class-based. While accepting much of the analysis of New Times, Rustin asserts that it is essential to remind ourselves that the fundamental division in society is between those who own capital and those who do not.

Post-Fordism also raises a set of important questions about the role of trade unions and the nature of modern employment. John Monks, Deputy General Secretary of the TUC, concedes to Mike Power in the fourth interview that the structural changes in the economy may well sound the death-knell for Keynesian style pump-priming. Monks argues, however, that full employment remains a critical goal for the trade union movement in the 1990s at a time when the unions find themselves in the paradoxical position of being held in higher popular esteem than they have for several decades and yet remain under relentless attack from the Tory government.

In the second section the attention shifts further to questions of economics, with Will Hutton, economics editor of the *Guardian* leading the discussion of the role of the trade unions into a wider consideration of Britain's economic and social problems. Hutton argues that the unions must look to lead the Labour Party into a new direction and that with socialism widely discredited, the unions will need to forge a new body of ideas of relevance to the 1990s. Pointing to the decline in unionisation and collective bargaining, Hutton describes an emergent stratification of British society between a third who are entirely marginalised and/or low paid, a third who are in a position of being 'newly insecure' and a third who are in secure, full-time jobs. The impacts of this social stratification are not only dramatic social ghettoisation, increasing social disintegration and rising crime but also gross inequalities of income which pose serious problems for economic recovery, since consumption patterns may not be sufficient to sustain production levels.

The issue of sustainable economic recovery is addressed in the next interview in this section where Stuart Wilks talks to William Keegan, economics editor of the *Observer*, about the state of the British economy. Speaking to Keegan just prior to the March 1993 budget and amid panic over the size of the Public Sector Borrowing Requirement, Wilks asks whether the economic problems of the 1990s are not a direct result of the policies of the 1980s. Keegan, a well-known critic of the monetarist policies of the previous decade and the pick 'n' mix policies of the current one, points to the critical structural problems in the British economy, notably the erosion of the tax base and the decimated manufacturing sector. Recovery, argues Keegan, will therefore have to be based on long-term planning, greater European cooperation and an appropriate relationship between the public and private sectors.

A different form of economic sustainability is addressed by environmental economist Michael Jacobs in his interview with Quentin Given. Jacobs points to a number of economic mechanisms which are available to promote sustainability, including using the tax system to shift consumption and production away from more environmentally damaging patterns, and also argues that technological advances can contribute to more ecologically sustainable production and energy consumption. Jacobs stresses the need for a shift in thinking about quality of life issues away from conventional concerns with standard of living based entirely on purchasing potential. But he remains highly conscious of the need to balance social and environmental concerns, and with reference to the examples of the coal industry and VAT on domestic fuel, argues that environmental objectives cannot be divorced from concern with the distribution of income and power in society.

Finally, Frank Blackaby presents a passionate case for the restoration of a full-employment policy. In a piece made consciously accessible for the lay person as well as for economists who, he feels, have lost sight of the main arguments of their own discipline, Blackaby argues that achieving full employment is largely a case of restoring the political will to do so. Blackaby first takes the reader through a quick lesson in what he terms 'kindergarten economics' before moving on to pull apart the cloudy thinking which he sees as the principal obstacle to achieving full employment. He then goes on to outline the policies and politics needed to bring unemployment down as quickly as it has risen in recent years. By arguing that 'it does not have to be like this' Blackaby's provocative piece will induce a reaction from all who read it.

Full employment as a cornerstone of the welfare state is a central part of the discussions in the third section on social justice. With 1993 marking the fiftieth anniversary of the Beveridge papers on full employment and the welfare state, Sir Gordon Borrie, chair of Labour's commission on social justice, makes the case for getting back to Beveridge. Borrie argues that full employment will be critical to the future of the welfare state since the extent of payments to the unemployed have come to undermine Beveridge's original conception. The need to get back to full employment is echoed by David Donnison who argues that if we are forced to accept present unemployment rates then 'progressives can go home and grow roses'. Mass unemployment is in danger of destroying the welfare state since it may make selective services and means testing necessary. Selective services, argues Donnison, will serve to destroy solidarity and make society more divisive. Optimistic that a progressive agenda will emerge to overcome the demoralisation on the left, Donnison warns, however, that it will not do just to seek to shepherd new political movements into the labour movement.

Mike Power's interview with Beatrix Campbell in the third chapter in this section addresses some of the problems of the old left approach to social policy and suggests some new directions for the left. Campbell sees that a key part of the crisis on the left has resulted from its dependence on the resources of the state, which has in turn led to an alienation from politics and from political parties. Arguing that the 1980s saw a fracturing of the notion that politics could make any difference to the lives of the poor and marginalised in society, Campbell posits that the left must accept that the incredible internal diversity of the 'working class' necessitates a new form of politics.

To round off this section on social policy issues, Steve Iliffe, a General Practitioner, pushes forward some ideas for a new agenda in the area of health care policy. Talking to Dom Ford, Iliffe admits that in many ways the left has been defeated but, he argues, the left still has the important capacity to argue the issues. The potential for a new agenda in health is there if the left can overcome its own conservatism. In particular, the left should be thinking more around ways of democratising areas such as health care policy.

A far-reaching democratisation of society is one possible project for the transformation of the left and section four looks in depth at the ideas of radical democracy. First, Adam Lent introduces radical democracy within the context of what he sees as a shrinking 'ideological menu'. Lent argues that two core issues of difference and inequality have grown enormously in importance in the postwar period while the classical political doctrines have become increasingly unable to deal with them. Outlining how issues such as race, gender, sexuality and lifestyle have led to the emergence of a diverse and fragmented new politics, Lent suggests that these new social movements can be forged, but never forced, into a new progressive agenda around the principles of radical democracy. He then proceeds to lay out the key political goals which these movements can seek to realise through radical democracy – those of extensive pluralism, differentiated citizenship and the achievement of complex equality.

This introduction to the ideas of radical democracy is then followed by interviews with some of the most renowned political theorists working in the subject area. Issues of equality and difference are taken up further in Anne Showstack Sassoon's conversation with Anne Coddington. Showstack Sassoon argues that concerns with equality must be reconciled with the realities of our differentiated and multifarious society. Not only do people vary as individuals; they also relate differently to society and to the state during different stages of their life. Therefore, Showstack Sassoon makes a case for a notion of equality and universalism in law and social policy which seeks to incorporate difference rather than ignoring it and imposing homogeneous and monolithic systems on a diverse citizenship.

In the next interview, Mike Power talks to Chantal Mouffe about the ideas of radical democracy and their relationship to socialist goals. Mouffe stresses that the socialism formulated largely in the nineteenth century fails to encompass fully concerns for relationships not based on economic relations, such as race and gender. The relevance of socialism, she argues, is in democratising as many social, political and economic relations as possible. The newly emergent social movements cannot be frog-marched into the labour movement. Instead, we should seek to build 'chains of equivalence' between different movements. Mouffe stresses that this cannot be achieved through imposition and that radical democracy is an ongoing process – it is not a model of society.

When asked by Adam Lent if there is a danger that radical democracy risks becoming an explain-all ideology, Ernesto Laclau is at pains to point out that radical democracy is not a blueprint. To a certain extent, Laclau does see radical democracy as an alternative to the traditional ideologies of the left (which he regards as being in crisis principally as a result of their failure to 'galvanise the imagination of the masses'). However, Laclau, like Mouffe, stresses that radical democracy is not an alternative to the liberal state but a force for change within it. Finally in this section, Geoff Mulgan talks to Noni Stacey about Demos, a new think tank intended to generate the radical ideas which, he suggests, political parties have become increasingly unable to offer. Mulgan argues that the great ideologies of socialism, conservatism and liberalism which he sees as essentially nineteenth-century constructs, still constitute the basis of our party system and much of our political debate as we approach the twenty-first century. Within this context, Mulgan sees Demos as being in a unique position to probe and promote radical ideas around the issues of citizenship and democratic control. For example, Mulgan suggests that the electorate could be given choices over government spending for core services such as health and education.

The fifth and final section of the book looks at some of the themes of the new politics, or, as it is described here, the 'nearly-new' politics. Jonathon Porritt and Quentin Given met just after the Rio summit to discuss the environmental agenda. Porritt confesses that he expected to be disappointed by Rio and admits that the kind of change required to guarantee a sustainable future will be a long time coming. In particular, he identifies critical problems in changing a system of thought which has, for centuries, dominated ideas about how best to meet human need and achieve economic success. However, Porritt sees many areas where progress can be made within the confines of current thought and practice, such as waste minimisation and more efficient use of resources, and goes on to suggest a number of ways in which the green movement can seek to make a more effective impact.

Ecology is also a major theme in the second interview, where Kate Soper argues a case for a redefinition of socialism around ecological principles. If socialism is to be revived, it must appear institutionally feasible but it must also be 'seductive', says Soper. This more seductive socialism would involve projecting an alternative vision to capitalism which breaks out of the obsession with measuring pleasure through material consumption. Soper adds that it will be necessary for socialism to transcend its class-based definition so that a socialist politics can emerge which engages the new social movements and which is imaginative in its content and style. The historical connection of socialism with class politics has become problematic since it tends to mean that newer issues of race, gender and ecology are treated as items to be added at the end of the 'laundry list'. While recognising that socialist politics are being revised around these issues Soper also points out that the new pluralism of the left is not a solution but very much the name of the problem.

In the next interview, Denise Searle talks to US feminist Shere Hite about her writings and about the position of the women's movement in the 1990s. The *Hite Report*s on sexuality, although initially well received in the 1970s, have come in for sterner and often cynical criticism in more recent years – a symptom of what Susan Faludi has termed 'backlash' (a term which Searle argues is a misnomer because it implies that women had somehow pushed *too* far, although she would not dispute the existence of what Faludi calls 'the undeclared war against American women' waged, in particular, by the US media). In spite of this climate, Hite sees that the women's movement is breaking through to a new era, detecting many signs of encouraging activity. Though clearly there is a long way to go – the American media, for example, provides ample evidence that men are still very much in control – and the only way to overcome this, argues Hite, is for women to break the taboo on anger which has restrained them in the past.

To conclude the book, Adam Lent talks to Stuart Hall about how the left can seek to reverse its apparent decline. Among other things, Hall advocates an intellectual exchange beyond the restricted discourse around the Labour Party and which focuses particularly on critical questions about developing new forms of state provision which avoid the old bureaucratic structures and of advancing a new language of universal citizenship which encompasses the multifarious claims and needs of our enormously diverse society. With the left facing a fourth consecutive Conservative term, Hall argues that the left must switch from defending the old agenda to constructing new visions which recognise the very real fears of different and also growing sections of society. Though by no means opposing the defensive role, Hall argues that having become locked into this position of defence, the left continues to ruin any attempts at renewal.

This book hopes to provide some ideas about how the left can switch from engaging in the increasingly futile defence of its old agenda to advancing the agenda which it has long neglected. Perhaps like too many before it, this is not a book concerned with providing definite answers but with beginning a serious search for them. However, this is by no means an idle search; it is necessarily a pro-active one. The turn of the century represents a watershed for the left and, given the current state of affairs, failure will be all too easy. This book is, we hope, one small step away from the direction of defeat.

PART ONE

SIFTING THE REMAINS OF THE SOCIAL DEMOCRATIC CONSENSUS:

LABOUR AND THE UNIONS IN THE 1990S

Seeking a Radical Party

David Marquand interviewed by **Nina Fishman**

Nina Fishman: How would you characterise the present relationship between leaders and led? Looking at the political culture and heritage of Europe and the US, it is possible to discern three interesting models. The first is the feudal, which arose in western Europe and contained a very solemn obligation of the leader towards the led. And one can argue that the British aristocratic Whigs [political party that after the 1688 Revolution aimed at subordinating the power of the crown to parliament, succeeded in the mid ninetenth century by the Liberals] were very much in that mode. Secondly, there are popular leaders who are of the people and who remain of the people. These include trade union leaders and some left political leaders. In this case the distinction between leaders and led becomes disguised. Thirdly, there is the '1848 model', where you have a bourgeois political thrust for liberty and freedom, which makes a bid for popular support and says it is acting on behalf of the people. But it is quite self-consciously able to take charge as a political class: much as the French political class have just done in terms of the Maastricht referendum.

David Marquand: I do not entirely agree with your models, although they are very interesting. In Britain today we have a kind of bankrupt Whiggery. It is a sort of noblesse oblige binding the leaders to the led, coupled with a certain sense of mutual obligation. The led have the duty to follow the leaders, but the leaders have the duty to act on behalf of the led and to respect and respond to them. And I suppose part of that model is that if the leaders do not behave appropriately then the led no longer have obligations to them. It contains an implicit contract. That has been the dominant mode of British political leadership for a long time. And the reasons are well known. For instance we have not had a revolution since the middle of the seventeenth century. Therefore we remained stuck in that essentially Whig-feudal model and never moved into your '1848 model' until very recent times.

The interesting thing is that the trade union inspired Labour Party was assimilated into this Whig-feudal model very quickly. However, the dominant Whig model began to break down recently, partly because of incompetence, real or perceived, on the part of the 'leaders'. They did not deliver the goods, Britain declined, and that undermined their legitimacy: people began to see that the emperor had no clothes. That is one factor. Secondly, the leaders have themselves started to lose confidence. This has occurred partly because of the experience of decline, but also for more profound reasons including cultural and economic change. One of the most remarkable features of post-war British history is the astonishing difference between the post-war Labour government, which was the final flowering of Whig leadership, and the Wilson government of the 1960s. The 1945 government had a breathtaking, existential self confidence. These were tough people, politically seasoned, who thought they had a right to govern and to expect the people to make sacrifices. They made some appalling mistakes early on, and in many respects theirs was not a very impressive government. They wasted vast sums of foreign exchange in the 1947 convertibility crisis and got some things very seriously wrong. But right up to the closing months of that government, you got the sense of a group of people with enormous confidence in their ability and right to rule, and to ask for public support – which, by and large, they got. In 1951 Labour got the largest popular vote in its history.

Contrast the Wilson government of the 1960s. It was better equipped in terms of personal qualifications: it was stuffed with people with firsts from the Oxford PPE school starting with Wilson himself. But it did not exude this extraordinary sense of inner self confidence. And a similar kind of decline can be traced in the Conservative Party. So by the 1970s the Whig model was in severe trouble. By the 1980s we see the appearance of a strange kind of bastard populism. In this the two most interesting figures, both emblematic of the 1980s, were Margaret Thatcher and David Owen. Both were populist in the sense that they based their claim to power on their intuitive sense of what the people wanted: on their ability to keep in tune with the innermost feelings of the people. They saw themselves as the embodiments of the popular will. They knew what the general will was, but not through reason. The denigration and humiliation that Margaret Thatcher inflicted upon the cabinet, and indeed the whole political elite, were remarkable instances of this. To her these were tiresome, boring figures who did not understand what the people really wanted.

But the trouble with this kind of populist leadership is that it is based on a misconception. The populist heroes do not incarnate the popular will. The populace may tolerate them for a while, but will not actually surrender their own emotions, values and preferences to an heroic kind of populist charismatic figure. There comes a really painful fall from grace when the heroic figure is knocked off the pedestal. Both Thatcher and Owen in their different ways had this very unpleasant experience at the end of the 1980s. So the problem now is that bankrupt Whiggery did not work, yet no one has offered a democratic alternative to it. The only alternative has been an equally bankrupt form of populism.

With the end of the cold war capitalism has not only been rampant but triumphant in terms of how it has been perceived worldwide. And returning to 1848 I would like to invoke the *Communist Manifesto* with Marx's references to the positive virtues of capitalism in unleashing the important forces of individualism against feudalism. Of course, as historians it is possible to see that such a sharp distinction between capitalism and feudalism was inaccurate, on the other hand there is validity in it. Do you consider capitalism, as we approach the end of the twentieth century, to be dynamic still and have the potential to be world changing?

This depends on which sort of capitalism you mean. This is the great question of present day politics, at least in industrial societies. What happened was extremely complex. Except for the early nineteenth century, capitalism was not particularly successful before World War II. Indeed, after the 1880s capitalism seemed to exhibit the critical symptoms that Marx had forecast. It was not, of course, the Marxist crisis in reality, but it looked as though it was and it was easily assimilated into Marxist categories. This is one reason why many idealistic and radical young people became communists, or fellow travellers, between the wars. It seemed to be both an accurate description and the only hopeful prescription for the future. But then in the contest between capitalism and communism, capitalism won.

However, this was not the capitalism of Marx or of the inter-war period. It was a peculiar, mixed economy, partly-socialised capitalism. This emerged after World War II in a series of 'second best compromises', all over Europe, and to a degree in North America. So what triumphed was not nineteenth century capitalism, still less inter-war capitalism. It was post-war capitalism, and that was a quite different animal. It was still based on private ownership of the means of production; it was still essentially a market economy, in which resources were allocated ultimately by the price mechanism. But it was a very different sort of capitalism, because it had been pushed into reforming itself precisely through its competition with communism. And that is the real irony and dilemma for us. Looking back on the immediate post-war period it seems grotesque that anybody should seriously have imagined that such a ghastly, appalling and incompetent regime as Stalin's could pose a serious security threat to western Europe. But that is not how people saw it in the 1940s. After all it was the Red Army that won the war: the Russian communist regime, even though led by an evil monster. And it seemed to Bevin and Attlee and the generation of leaders who created the European Community in the late 1940s and early 1950s, that communism might triumph in Germany, and that if it did so then it would triumph throughout Europe, because Germany was the key to Europe. These considerations were a critical element in the US response to the problems of western Europe at the time.

The US Marshall Plan, was sometimes interpreted as a form of Rooseveltian New Deal designed to save the American economy from its own contradictions. That may be partly true, but it was not the critical factor. The critical factor was that by 1947, when Marshall made his famous speech, the Americans had concluded that Bevin was right and that there was a serious threat from the Soviet Union. Against their original predilections they therefore accepted essentially social-democratic forms of capitalism to fend off the threat of communism.

Now the great question is: with the threat removed, and a triumphalist neo-liberal return to the nineteenth century carrying all before it in the west, will capitalism stay reformed? With the Soviet pressure off, so to speak, with the Russians queuing up for western handouts, seeking to remodel their own economy in the monetarist image and looking to very debased and simplified models of western capitalism, will western capitalism stay reformed? That is the gut question of our time.

That is very useful because all too often that question is not even uttered *sotto voce* – it remains unsaid because this triumphant capitalism is so much in the ascendant.

Exactly. We can argue about the extent to which the long economic boom was a product of reformed social-democratic welfare capitalism, and the extent to which it was a product of economic circumstances that would have worked their way through irrespective of what kind of regime was in power. But we will never solve that problem because you do not have controlled experiments in history. What matters is that there was a long boom, low unemployment, reasonable rates of inflation and stable exchange rates, which now makes the 1950s and 1960s seem like a golden age. Compare this to the present situation, which is in many ways reminiscent of the tormented, incompetent and inefficient form of capitalism that existed in the 1920s and 1930s. We have upheavals in the exchange rates, repetitive devaluations, mass unemployment, which nobody knows how to cope with; and the Keynesian economic remedies, which seemed to be so successful in the postwar period, turn out to be inoperable.

Right, and that is the question. In some ways it is knowing the right questions to ask that enables us to think our way through to possible solutions.

Sure, and it is an immensely complicated question which is essentially a question of political economy. It is not primarily an economic question. It is: what kind of regime, in the very broadest sense, is necessary? Part of the problem is that we do not have a model of reformed capitalism. This became clear to me talking to Russians and East Europeans. They know that the command economy has collapsed, and that it was grotesquely irrational as well as horrible in human and political terms. Now they want eco-

nomic success, but where do they look for the model that will produce it? They find a vacuum. There is no theorised model of
reformed capitalism. There are plenty of descriptive accounts of
what happened in different countries, but they will not help a
Hungarian, Pole or Russian looking for 'the handbook that will
tell me what to do'.

**This leads perfectly into the next question. You are absolutely
right that the question is political economy, and not straight economics. And the long post-war boom was in many ways prepared by the 1939-45 war economy and that what we are looking for in a reformed, post-war capitalism is a proper, reasonable
balance between the individual and the collective. If that balance
is not in equilibrium then you either get the command economy
at one extreme or the neo-liberal at the other. So, what do you
consider ought to be the balance between the individual and the
collective, and where do we stand now?**

That question cannot be answered a priori. And maybe it is part of
the problem that we tend to think there is, or ought to be, an a priori answer. Consider the two polar opposites, the command economy, on the one hand and the mythological, individualistic free market on the other. Both have a doctrine, based upon an extremely
simplified view of society. That is why they are easily understood
and why both of them have a certain aesthetic beauty about them.
If you accept the premises of Marxism, or of individualistic free
market liberalism, then the whole system hangs together. That is
why both are so seductive to many very clever people.
Unfortunately, they are wrong. But they are not wrong because
there is a better answer somewhere, of which these are only glim-
mering approximations: they are wrong because it is not possible to
produce a comprehensive model of society and history and where it
is going. What has really happened is that eighteenth-century ratio-
nalism has collapsed. And along with it has gone its belief that
somewhere, if only we were clever enough, and learned enough, and
did enough hard work, we could discover the secret of the universe.
The real problem is that there ain't no such thing. There is no alternative except the very boring one of muddling through, with a bit
of this and a bit of that: a trial and error approach to politics.

What you are really saying is that ours is a post-enlightenment

rather than post-modern era. It is perfectly reasonable to say that it took two centuries after the French revolution for this extraordinarily potent thing to work itself through. However it may have finally done so, and that is one reason why there is no such thing as a proper balance between the individual and the collective. We have to find our balance in each new circumstance and we cannot allow ourselves to answer that question a priori.

That's right. But in a way this relates to our earlier conversation about leadership. To contemplate all this honestly it is necessary to be pessimistic. What are you telling people? What is your message? What is the bottom line? Well the bottom line is that there is no bottom line – things are bloody difficult. There is no marvellous all-embracing answer. In this situation the populist alternative has some attraction. At least it can say: well this is what I am going to do. And so, I think, does your '1848 model', though in a different kind of way. This other approach has lost its resonance.

Now you and I are both committed to the further development of the European Community, but how can Europe develop while the politicians in Europe are unwilling to take risks?

That is a very good way of putting it. However the really striking contrast in the 1940s was that British politicians were not prepared to take the risks which their continental counterparts took. France, for example, had grown used to very high protective tariffs since the seventeenth century, and the whole tradition of the French political economy was protectionist. For it to accept free competition with the industrial might of Germany was an extraordinary political risk for the weak governments of the Fourth Republic, yet they took it. You had a courageous political elite in all the major European countries; and the great paradox of the EC is that because they took these risks, they produced the most successful period of European history since god-knows-when, and thereby undermined the conditions of their success. For success has come to be taken for granted. We have come to assume that some divine law says there will never again be a war between France and Germany, that we will enjoy the fruits of economic interdependence for ever, that our success was not the result of amazing creativity and willingness to take risks on the part of the political elite, but automatic and inevitable. Sometimes we even think we can afford to imperil it; and of course we cannot. I sense your groping for the question: why can't we have the same willingness to take risks now, and how do we get a political leadership prepared to take the same sort of risks because they face just as big a crisis? Well, I do not know the answer. Maybe the truth about the post-war period is that people are prepared to be courageous only in extremis. And perhaps the difference is that today's difficulties appear to be manageable without courageous decisions, while in the 1940s people had their backs against the wall.

Finally, can we talk about the Labour Party? Is it finished as a radical political party? Has it been unable to make the transition from being an old socialist party to the new radical party that it needs to do?

It is too soon to say; the jury is still out. I left the Labour Party in the 1980s hoping to replace it with a Social Democratic Party modelled on the German social democrats. Well you know what happened to the SDP. The Labour Party picked itself up, dusted itself down, and became social democratic, as opposed to the busted flush of old style socialism. But the trouble was that it became social democratic just as social democracy itself was becoming a busted flush. And so having made the transition from socialism to social democracy, which it has very nearly made, the question now is: can it make the transition from social democracy, of a small 'c' conservative kind, to being the radical party that the times need? One test case is its attitude to the state. This is sometimes talked of in terms of constitutional reform. But the significance and importance of constitutional reform is what it really tells you about people's attitude to the state.

The Labour Party came onto the scene before World War I, when arguments about the nature of the state were at the centre of political debate, and when the liberals of that era were trying to modernise the state. But then after World War I, when it became the major left of centre party in the two party system, it accepted the British state as the vehicle for its policies. This was the great historic tragedy of the British left. The Labour Party favoured proportional representation (PR) before the World War I and abandoned it afterwards. Labour also favoured Scottish home rule before the war. It was led by a Scot, Ramsay MacDonald, who believed strongly in home rule, and in Scottish nationhood and identity. But it abandoned all of those things because it wanted to win power within the existing system, to use state power to alleviate poverty and hardship, and to socialise the means of production. These were seen as the serious and real issues, whereas the structure of the state was a trivial, second order question. And so it has been trapped in a contradiction throughout its history.

The party that believed in reconstructing society wished to do so by and through a bankrupt state; and that was *always* an absurdity. But people who pointed this out were regarded as cranks and troublemakers. This attitude lasted until the 1960s. Even in the 1980s, despite its adoption of social democracy as opposed to socialism on economic and social matters, the party was still hung-up about the state. In the last General Election, Labour had a much more radical programme on the state than ever before. But this package has never been presented in a radical way; it is presented as a series of piecemeal tinkerings. They buy off the Scots with devolution. But if there is going to be devolution in Scotland they face the problem of the English regions. That means regional government. Then there is the Bill of Rights. They had to come up with something, but it was a mishmash of nonsense. And, as there was pressure for proportional representation among potential supporters, Labour set up a commission, and at the last minute in the election started to flirt with PR. Not surprisingly it looked bloody stupid and alienated many voters. So the question of whether it could be a really radical party hinges on whether it can develop a project for the reconstitution of the British state as part of a united Europe. If it cannot do that it will not be the sort of party that is needed. Yet there is no alternative to the Labour Party. If you have my views, you find yourself in an extraordinarily unsatisfactory situation. I desperately want Labour to be the radical party that is needed: I am not convinced that it is going to be, but I cannot see anybody else being it either. The Liberal Democrats, who are radical on the state and its relationship to a united Europe, are retreating into the past, in a very stupid and reactionary way, on economic policy. They are completely failing to address the key questions about the nature of modern capitalism. They are becoming increasingly neo-liberal in their economic thinking, which is exactly what we do not need. Moreover, the blunt fact is that we live in a system in which third parties have very little chance and the Alliance blew the chance they had. It had two goes, very nearly succeeded, but it failed. And in the last General Election the Labour Party gained votes – not enough to win – but at least it gained; and the Liberal Democrats lost. They are now in the same position as the Liberals were in 1974. That is better than their position in the 1960s, but it is not a tremendous success story to be in 1992 where you were in 1974.

Reviving Socialism

Michael Meacher interviewed by **Mike Power.**

Mike Power: In *Diffusing Power: The Key to Socialist Revival* (London: Pluto, 1992) you talk about the need for decentralisation. But there seems to be a contradiction as you come at these issues from a parliamentary, statist tradition. And you talk about seeking a 'socialist' renewal, while for most people the word 'socialism' has unacceptable connotations, which arise from the East European example, and from centralised, nationalised, undemocratic practices of statist welfarism. For many it also meant an end to diversity and difference, and favoured a universalistic 'common good', which required people to subsume their individualism and identity. My reading of your book is that you have not moved far from these ideas and go only half way towards empowerment of people and then stop, because you seem to be defending an out-of-date socialist 'big idea'.

Michael Meacher: The picture of socialism that you paint is that which is given by our opponents, who want to link it with totalitarianism in Eastern Europe and all the sins of Stalin, Gosplan, centralised bureaucracy, and who also identify it with red tape, man in Whitehall knows best, and lack of freedom and pluralism. But socialists have never seen it in that way. For me socialism is inalienably linked with freedom, and Eastern Europe was never anything to do with socialism. But it is also about concern for others, for justice, and against poverty. So socialism is not dead. Our problem is that in Britain we have never seen a way towards a non-statist pluralist socialism. In the 1940s socialism was synonymous with nationalisation, which was seen as the cutting edge of efficiency as against the waste of pre-war unemployment and capitalist failure. The state took responsibility. But nationalisation was far too centralist and concentrated in Whitehall; it was run by bureaucrats and private managers, not by ministers, and little changed. I still favour public ownership in many areas, not least water and the basic utilities, the nuclear industry as long as we have it, and of course, services such as health. But there has to be a decentralisation of power and it is my fundamental theme that it has never been given a chance to develop.

So what are your philosophical and theoretical antecedents? You say in your book that we are in a new economic situation where new political imperatives are required. There is little doubt that political parties are weaker, the trades unions are on their backs, mass production and organisations and movements are also weaker. So, in this post-Fordist situation with a more atomised society with politics geared more towards consumption than production, how can your ideas, that still seem to promote the 'common good', and which appear to run counter to your description of society, remain valid?

There are two fundamental changes. One is the shift from industrial mass production, from centralised planning and monolithic services, and, as you say, society is more atomised. The big development is the microchip; that opened up the possibility for a more tailor-made, specialised, flexible relationship between the producer and the buyer. Therefore specialised needs have grown and producers can increasingly meet them, almost on a daily basis. Secondly, socialism was about protecting the general good, the poorest, creating opportunity and fair shares. In post World War II western societies some two-thirds were pretty poor. There was always a ruling class and the only way the two-thirds could secure their rights was to band together. That is where trade union and working class, community and urban solidarity arose from. But as people's living standards improved, roughly during the quarter century – 1948 to1973 – this was seen to be achieved on an individualist basis. And we now have the 'one-third two-thirds' society, but with the two-thirds being better off, albeit with clear evidence of a new under-class. For the new two-thirds their ideology, communal responses and attitudes to solidarity have changed. But we should not attempt to resurrect the old communal solidarity and past truisms on which socialism was born. Instead, we should seek the essence of the socialist project, which was to protect the weak and provide opportunities, but on an individual rather than collectivist basis. Individuals need a job, a home, opportunities for training, and redress against poor public services – and these individual wants are fraying at the edges. So I argue for empowerment and realise that cannot be achieved through collectivist means.

But you provoke me to ask again: why saddle yourself with the designation socialism? After all, despite your disclaimers about Eastern Europe, what is needed now is to redefine socialism rather than revive it.

I have a great affection for the socialist idea and am against jettisoning the whole concept, not out of nostalgia but because it really does mean social justice, fair play and for want of a better term 'brotherhood of man'. These remain vibrant symbols of an alternative vision. Collectivism was historically a means to an end and not synonymous with socialism. Therefore, changing from a centralised to a decentralised economy the same dichotomy arises, because a decentralised economy is no more necessarily capitalist than a centralised one is socialist. I see a socialist decentralised economy as one in which power has been shifted to whatever is the appropriate forum among ordinary people. This may be workers in the factory or service users with different mechanisms designed to put power into their hands. That shift away from the traditional holders of power to the mass of the people is a shift from capitalism to socialism. And that is my vision.

But many people would say to you – yes, of course, that is what we would expect a member of the shadow cabinet to say after you have just lost a general election. Your party is in a mess, and although 35 per cent of the vote was an improvement it was pretty pathetic under the circumstances of economic crisis, and the Tories in an apparently weak position. Labour presented a voter-friendly face with policies to match, but you still lost and have even less chance of winning next time following the constituency boundary changes, a Tory engineered economic recovery and maybe even a new leadership. So you are really doing no more than 'tarting up' the party policy to give it a new image, build its membership so that you can become a single party government again. But that empowers nobody except the parliamentary Labour Party and the Labour leadership.

I would have a lot a of sympathy with that view if we were just putting forward a lot of rhetoric, using it to ride to power and then intending to drop it. I would utterly despise such an approach, and I am serious about what I say. There is nothing wrong with seeking power and on that I agree with Neil Kinnock. But we must not only seek power. After all, you cannot do anything until you get power, but it is useless to have the party in power if it does not fundamentally improve the lot of the people, particularly the poorest. Labour must have a serious message. We did lose a fourth time, and not just by a whisker, but by a whopping seven-and-a-half per cent. This was not to do with tax, the tabloid hysteria, or the Sheffield rally, but because people no longer saw the Labour Party as standing for anything. We lacked a clear, sharp message presenting a different and better society. That is the only way the left can win. In 1945 we did, saying never again shall we have the 1930s. And in 1964 we won on the idea of the 'white heat of the technological revolution'. These were new, fresh, vibrant and transforming approaches. Today Labour is not believed as it appears consensual, ultra respectable and despite all the talk about taking on the vested interests it is not serious about power. You do not go to the City for swish dinners with the people you really intend to take on.

You did not mention Labour's programme in 1983, which was the most far reaching of all. It included the 'redistribution of the balance of wealth and power in favour of the working people and their families' and much more. But Labour crashed to its worst defeat in decades.

The 1983 manifesto was old socialism, and although I agree with the aims, they were not fresh. But despite that the real reason why we lost was nothing to do with the manifesto. It followed internecine warfare in the Labour Party on a scale never previously seen. The right and left fought daily battles in the media denigrating each other, and as a result the party halved its position in the polls during 1981 and never recovered.

One reason that the Tories can win is that they have the advantage of a corrupt electoral system, and they can win with 58 per cent against them, but still get a 21 seat majority.

But while there is an anti-Tory majority there is an even bigger anti-Labour one. In three-party politics no one gets an overall majority as first-past-the-post weights it in favour of the one with its nose in front. Therefore the Tories have a legitimate right to be in power.

However, the non-Tory majority certainly had non-Tory policies, there was little difference between Labour and Lib-Dem manifestoes.

But that strengthens my point that we do not stand for anything significantly different. We have to now establish our position and convey clearly that we really mean it.

Though if you do stand for something significantly different would you not then find yourself representing an even smaller minority?

No. We are not simply sloganising about attacking the bosses or separating ourselves from the establishment. The real point is to make ourselves an effective champion of the skilled working and lower middle classes who are the centre of gravity of British politics. We have to make them feel that we are economically competent and that we will advance their interests, not just by redistribution, but by empowerment and giving them an opportunity to call the shots.

But you have a big problem here. You speak of classes when we are moving towards a situation where, for instance, the current two million homeworkers are expected to become eight million by the end of the century. Therefore, people are less communitarian and do not work together, which means the basis on which you predicate your 'class' approach to empowerment is inappropriate and falling apart quicker than you give it credit for.

I am not absolutely sure of that. It is true that workplaces are getting smaller, but there are still some big, powerful and immensely important companies, and I would not rule out public ownership in some of those cases. However, it is true that a third to a half of Britain's workers will soon be in companies of less than 20 people. That means empowerment in the workplace, and they are still vulnerable to the vagaries of the market – a company is closing in Britain every six minutes. So trades unions are still very relevant, even though they still have to change their ways of working. Yes, working structures are changing, but so must the means of redress. Consumers of services were always atomised. Single mothers who need pre- or post-natal services and nursery places have always had housing and income problems – we must find effective ways to reach out to such people.

How will Labour help such people? Empowerment seems to be the key to any future left strategy. This means individuals in any collective they are involved in reflecting a new radical citizenship and their own autonomy and interests, while respecting other people's rights and needs. What role can Labour really play in this? After all, people are feeling their oppression as emerging not merely, or even mainly, from the labour/capital contradiction, but from social oppression such as racism and sexism. And to try to get them all under the Labour banner to get their votes would be disastrous. In this situation, with such a diversity of opinion and needs, is it not irresponsible for Labour to be saying we will not even contemplate an alliance?

There is nothing wrong with campaigning to win votes. What is wrong is to use policies to win electoral support every five years and then ignoring those policies. That is deeply disillusioning. My book is a personal statement of the need to 'diffuse power' as the essential and dynamic characteristic of a left transforming party; it offers many ideas that the party could advance and seek committed backing. For instance, I favour using referenda, including one on the Maastricht treaty, and also on local issues where a single party has overwhelming control, whether Labour in Oldham or the Tories in Basingstoke. I also include new approaches to employment and services. But Labour has still to go through a big conversion before we get close to this. On the issue of alliances it is too early to say that Labour will not win the next election. However, if we do not have any new ideas and just try to cobble the two parties together on the grounds that the Lib-Dems 18 per cent and Labour's 35 per cent will give us a winning 53 per cent, then it will not work – a deal from on high will not do the job. We have to find a new way of enthusing the hearts and minds of our potential supporters. Furthermore, I hope that people will pick up these ideas for their own sake. In that sense, I am in no way simply pushing the interests of Labour. The Labour Party is a husk; we are steadily going down. Membership is at 260,000, just

60,000 above the Liberals. We are about two-thirds of one per cent of the voting population and that is absolutely pathetic. We are a party of diehards who are interested in politics and that figure shows that we are totally failing to win the hearts and minds of the broad mass of people. My book is a contribution to the Labour Party beginning to do that.

New Directions for Labour

Mike Rustin interviewed by **Kevin Davey**

Kevin Davey: In your book, *For a Pluralist Socialism,* (London: Verso, 1985) which was a response to the 1979 and 1983 election defeats, you argued in favour of participatory democracy in the Labour Party, a commitment to proportional representation and the development of a programme that would win the political centre ground for Labour. Others on the left took one or two elections longer to reach the same conclusions. Do you still hold the views that you expressed then?

Mike Rustin: We start from a much weaker position now. When those essays were written the idea of devising a reasonably radical, but cautiously stated programme was appropriate. Since then we have been pretty comprehensively defeated and putting together a moderate programme of social advance is no longer the starting point. We need to diagnose what the opportunities are and also what weaknesses exist in the governing structure. These are analytic rather than programmatic problems. What I suggested before presupposed there was still a powerful base for sealing a kind of coalitionist, progressive middle class and working class politics. It would be unwise to assume that such an entity any longer exists, so we have to start somewhere else. I am affected in this by my experiences of Charter 88 and its failure to make electoral reform part of a larger package uniting collective liberalism and social democracy. No one has even started to talk about that.

It was the emphasis which you had placed on a discourse of rights which led to your involvement in the launch of Charter 88. Yet just before the last election you said that the Charter's failure to demand a commitment to economic and social rights from its supporters had set the definition of citizenship back a century. The initiative on this does seem to have passed over to supporters of the Social Chapter, Labour, the Institute for Public Policy Research (IPPR) and Liberty. Why is it that Charter 88 has not embraced the notion of social rights? And how does this affect prospects for electoral reform?

In a sense Charter 88 missed the boat. They had the chance to widen the agenda to include economic and social rights and they should have done so. Instead they resisted it quite strongly. They have adopted an exceedingly old fashioned agenda. But they have not moved anyone else's agenda back. However, it is bizarre to couch citizenship in such legal terms. Proportional representation is important, but it is no longer vital, certainly not in terms of defeating Thatcherism. Even in terms of Labour getting re-elected I am not sure how much it matters. Labour's most rational strategy would probably be to promise reform after the next election. In other words, they would try and force the Liberals to support them by saying we promise to legislate within one year, and they would try to increase their legitimacy by being in office. That is the most they can offer anyway because they cannot introduce reform before they get into power.

Following Bill Clinton's election success, some in the Labour Party are now looking to the Democrats as a model for the policy changes and bold presentation that are deemed essential to election victory here. Is the political wind now going to blow from the west? What difference will the Clinton presidency make to British politics?

As Labour is less tied by its traditional base, because there is not a traditional base in quite the same sense anymore, it is prompted to look for the broadest range of support. And it is no longer impossible for it to find it on its own. The Democrats in America had the same problem but have managed to restore a successful coalition by moving substantially towards the centre and remodelling themselves as a modern interventionist party. Labour will do the same, unless the Tories manage to do it first, which is another possibility. If Labour tries it could succeed. However, it will not happen if the Tories manage to regenerate themselves on Clinton-type lines, with an appropriate leader and an appropriately reformist package, stealing quite a lot of Labour's clothes, and engineering some kind of recovery. I once thought that would happen, but now the Tories appear to be doomed to a hollowed out existence until they crumble.

We should not get too starry eyed about the Clinton project. The main thing is that there is a bunch of highly competent, new style social democrats in power after many years of reaction. They should not be regarded as soul brothers and we should not look for too many parallels between their policy programme and ours. But they provide an example. A precedent could seen in the interplay between Reaganism and Thatcherism, which went in both directions. Thatcher offered a modern and strong leadership which impressed the new 'US social democrats'. But most of the intellectual work which led to that programme was done in the US rather than Britain. Also one remembers Kennedy and the various attempts by Wilson to echo his modernisation programmes over here.

To be certain one would have to know more about the mental furniture of the quite small elite that determines Labour Party policy making. Who are their advisers? The number of people Smith and Brown listen to is actually quite small. These public relations people, electoral theorists, academic advisers and journalists go back and forwards across the Atlantic making it their business to find out what is going on, make friends inside the party and lock into what is happening. If, for example, Clinton introduces an employment programme that involves some element of Work Fare, an obligation to work or carry out some form of community service, it would be very surprising if that did not rapidly become big news in England as a potential way of dealing with unemployment. Party researchers and think tanks would pick it all up. That is how great the impact of the Americans on English speaking countries is. The current Labour leadership is more intellectually confident than Kinnock was and it will be less factional about who it talks to and will be more willing to allow these ideas to move around. Although they are obviously in no great hurry and they have an extraordinarily slow game plan, they will try to create some kind of intellectual sustenance as time goes by.

You were a critic of the New Times argument that a post-Fordist economy based on information technology was transforming

production, consumption, the forms of social organisation and social identities.[1] You said that it claimed too much too soon and that this new form of production could co-exist with older social and economic arrangements, some of which the left should defend. Five years on, whose argument looks the stronger?

The most important point is that the attack on old fashioned class politics in the New Times position obscures the fact that what we are suffering from is a form of class politics. What is going on *is* a class strategy, not a simple set of technological changes. It is primarily the response of capital to the resistances posed by the welfare state, trade unionism and a culture of equality. Disorganised capitalism is what capitalism does to get around the organisations that are set up to resist it or to negotiate with it. It is an extraordinary idea that we are living in a world devoid of class, when you have got the most determined class politics in anybody's memory grinding away at all the institutions that were formerly the bases of resistance. There was a degree of animosity towards the traditional left in those positions. What was actually being implied and felt in those disputes was the argument that it was the traditional left that got us into this mess. That was overestimated. While there obviously were left wing excesses, they were never of any great importance. Symbolically, there was the miners' strike, and governments were defeated. But the left was not exactly a massive force. There was a balance of class power that resulted in real difficulties for the dominant system, but that was not the left's doing, that was a result of citizenship demands which the population had established.

There is an element of self hatred in the New Times critique of traditional left positions. Having said that, the analysis of what was changing and the new forms of production, consumption, welfare, communication, all that was absolutely spot on. Those things are happening and they have profound implications that we have to take very seriously. The agenda that we have to cope with is a globalised one, that is where the real processes are taking place and if we do not address that we are wasting our time. The observation that a different set of social relations is eroding traditional solidarity is also right. Capitalism has succeeded in dividing the constituencies that it had formerly created, industrial workers and mass consumers and all the rest of it; that certainly makes a big difference to us and any new politics has to take account of it.

So in a way I have many agreements with the New Times analysis and what it means for the construction of a programme. But the real division is still between those who own the capital and those who do not. That is what generates inequality. That argument is not very prominent in New Times as a position, where it is regarded as too old fashioned, fundamentalist and classist. Why is it that the people who grasp that fundamental relationship find themselves denying that anything has changed, while the people who find themselves saying everything has changed deny this fundamental theory?

You have argued in your recent work that psychoanalytic ideas can enrich socialist thought and practice. To some extent that is pushing at an open door. The development of Freud's work in the sphere of linguistics by Jacques Lacan, for example, has had a major impact on cultural theory and feminism. But instead you have chosen to celebrate the work of Melanie Klein and her successors in the British Object Relations school which focuses on child development and process of separation from adults. What is at stake here politically?

There is a danger that socialists will hold an unconsidered, shallow or merely utopian view of human beings and their underlying dimensions. One of the great virtues of the psychoanalytic tradition is that it does actually have some grasp of the experience of pain; of separation, negativity, envy and anxiety. We must too. So one of the reasons for taking psychoanalysis seriously is simply a commitment to a certain kind of psychological realism.

Secondly, there is a connection between the morality of the welfare state, ethical socialism and psychoanalysis. There were also actual historical connections. For example, the development of the child psychoanalytic tradition was concerned with the notion of public support for the development of children and families, and it extended into care for the dying and the treatment of people suffering from all kinds of psycho-social difficulties, stress, trauma and child abuse.

Common to all of this is an emotionally textured and subtle grasp of pain. Sometimes it is socially produced pain, sometimes it is psychologically produced pain. The English socialist tradition has always been concerned about pain: in a way this has been one of its primary focuses. And the Kleinian tradition has been on the front line engaging with the particular and specific qualities of social and psychological pain.

The third reason is that as we move into a more complex society, so the agenda and specification of what counts as a reasonable standard of life goes up. Not to be hungry is no longer enough. Even not dying before you are 65 is not enough. People worry about what their quality of life is going to be like, even what the quality of death is going to be like. We develop a more complex set of aspirations and needs.

Psychoanalysis and its various social applications actually do address those dimensions of our existence. They provide a relevant kind of practice and training. The aspects that are most relevant socially are the applications in the fields of public health, psychotherapy and social care. That is, for example, realising in a children's ward that the relationship between a mother and baby is the most important thing that is going on and not the timetable of feeding and changing. The English clinical tradition is a good deal more helpful in this respect than Jacques Lacan. He addresses a different kind of problem, that is about identity and the loss of a solid sense of self, which provides a language to address states of extreme cultural and psychological confusion. It does provide a powerful and interesting language for dealing with that, but it does not address questions of pain, remedy, cure and intervention very well. My reason for being interested is not that I regard it as the centre of socialism. I am interested in Kleinian thought and I am also interested in socialist ideas, and these things are connected.

1. See *New Times: The Changing Face of British Politics in the 1990s*, Stuart Hall and Martin Jacques (eds.) London: Lawrence and Wishart/Marxism Today, 1989.

THE UNIONS' NEW AGENDA

John Monks interviewed by **Mike Power**

Mike Power: What should be the objectives of individual trade unions and the Trades Union Congress (TUC) in helping Britain's economic recovery? In the 1960s and 1970s, the Economic Committee of the TUC had the key to number 10 Downing Street, and talks were held. But such high level meetings no longer take place. So what are the key policy elements for the unions in terms of growth, employment, development, the environment and the social market?

John Monks: For trade unions the new agenda is similar in some respects to the old one. It starts with the level of employment. The TUC has decided to dedicate itself to re-raising the issue of full employment, and not to accept the established wisdom that it is impossible to return to the full employment concept which dominated British economic policy up until the mid 1970s. In those days we were worried about 600,000 unemployed. The number one trade union objective is to do something about unemployment, and to redress the sense of hopelessness that we can't do anything about it and will always have a massive pool of unemployed. There is currently talk in some Labour circles about a Full Employment Commission, and some of the churches are saying that full employment needs to be revived. There's a long way to go and it would be wrong to pretend it will be easy within a very competitive world economy.

What does this mean though? Full employment doesn't mean the same today as it did in the 1970s. We're not in a situation where the corrupted version of Keynesian economic fine-tuning, which was applied after World War II, can be used to rush everybody back into jobs. If you are concerned about the nature of growth and the environment, and we recognise that we're in a post-Fordist situation where high technology industry has become more important; then the nature of employment and the kind of full employment that you are seeking is going to be very different. Are you, therefore, looking at ideas like basic income schemes?

The situation is different for all the reasons you have described. Therefore, the solution is not likely to be people rushing off to work in factories that have suddenly got full order books prompted by big government spending. However, if the location of the work has changed, and the kind of opportunities are quite different for most people, then the idea of linking people to the work that needs to be done is very important. Nowadays very few young people go to work in factories, but all around us there is a vast amount of work that needs to be done, therefore full employment is as valid as ever. The solution is not just pump-priming the economy through macroeconomic policies, because a lot of money could go to people who are doing quite well, while people in the inner cities, or who are disadvantaged, are then left out. It is therefore a question of targeting assistance, and spending and intervening much more sensitively. Once full employment is established as a key objective it is then possible to harness the nation's energies behind it and target particular work projects and areas of development. These can include improving the environment, and refurbishment rather than massive redevelopments: then it is possible to see ways of putting people back to work.

Could you say something about the article you wrote in *Personnel Management* in 1992, in which you talked about the Japanese model as against the UK. Japanese companies are large scale, for example motor cars, although niche production slightly reduces the scale. None the less, what you discovered on your visit to Japan, and what you wrote about, is how Japanese companies are more concerned about human resources than they are about capital resources. This is important, but some people have criticised it by saying that instead of taking the old slogan of 'People before profit' you are now saying 'People make profit'. So, if all you do is admire or celebrate that kind of management, you are just agreeing to a change in emphasis. How do you feel about that?

I certainly was not intending to celebrate Japanese management, although some press stories gave that impression. But you cannot underestimate their achievements both in Japan and in Britain. Most British workers who work for these companies like it, and these are leading-edge world companies in key markets like motors and electronics. Most workers also feel that they have opportunities which they perhaps did not have with their previous employers. So we have got a lot to learn, and the lessons are not that strange. Many British companies always knew a lot about what Japanese companies were doing, but the difference is that they apply it more systematically and in a more disciplined way. And there is no doubt that the Japanese can be criticised on a number of important counts. For example, working time is too long; their interest in environmental questions is lacking in a number of important respects; and they are Fordist in mentality in that they look for never-ending growth for the purchase of their goods. In Japanese human resource management there is a smack of authoritarianism, even of totalitarianism. Their approach is that workers will be communicated with and involved in discussion about how to do the job, and given scope to get on with it, but only within certain strongly defined boundaries. Their rights to challenge or to have any democratic say are virtually nil. One job for the unions is to find our niche in their world. This could give workers a degree of representation and a right to a say. Greater industrial democracy and high quality production is needed. If Britain is to be able to afford to be a successful and generous society, both towards its own citizens and towards those in the developing world, we have got to have a big quality sector, both in goods and services.

Let's now talk about the unions in the 1990s. This government is incredibly unpopular, and the anti-Tory mood is hardening with more potential Tory voters saying that they would vote for a Lib-Lab alliance. This was also revealed around the miners' anti-pit closure campaign, and actions against redundancy. But the problem faced by the unions is that the hard, sectarian left is calling for general strikes, when there is no ground swell for such action and this simply alienates people. On the other hand it is also possible to be over cautious, with only token responses. Do we not need a strategy in between these two approaches?

The unions have to have a number of responses. The TUC is not only detecting a lot of frustration and fear, but also a determination to fight and not be pushed around. And this is so particularly in sectors where unemployment is not so immediate. People are saying, 'How much worse can things get', and more are now looking towards the unions for some protection and a lead. Where there are disputes over jobs, security or pay then more workers are preparing to have a go, and are considering strike action. Politically, strike actions will not necessarily lose popular support. Although they may provide an excuse for some Tory back-benchers, who in the excitement of the public outrage at what Heseltine announced, linked themselves to the 'coal group' to get out of their previous commitment. But in the community at large few people will condemn miners for striking for their pits and jobs. Apart from the one-off responses the challenge to us is to harness people's different fears and worries about the labour market behind a coherent alternative approach. The TUC is seeking to establish a full employment forum to bring together all those people who do not see the issue as a distant echo of the 1960s. We want to involve a wide spectrum of the community in the forum, including prominent employers, voluntary and religious organisations, all sitting with the unions to grapple with this crucial question.

Would this become a central campaigning theme for the TUC over a fairly long period?

Yes. We have two time scales. In the medium term, we are asking, can Britain earn its living in the world? Can we provide the quality products that people want? In the immediate future the issue is: what do we do about the three million unemployed? What useful opportunities can we devise for them? The TUC has good experience in this area. Consider the former Manpower Services Commission, which ran quite popular schemes, and compare this with today when the cost per head in each scheme is getting less and less. These cuts are due to government adjustments in the Public Sector Borrowing Requirement. However, the TUC will campaign for quality schemes and training courses.

Will this campaign be linked to the Labour Party's bandwagon or will it be directed throughout society and the whole political establishment, to enable you to put pressure on governments, of whatever persuasion?

I see this approach as being across society, although there will undoubtedly be many points of similarity with Labour's programme. But in the TUC we are deeply conscious of the fact that we have got to influence all parts of society and all shades of mainstream political opinion. We have to win support across the community, and it is when trade unions unite their members regardless of politics that they are most successful. It was that approach that stopped Heseltine in his tracks last October, when people in Cheltenham, as well as in the coalfield communities, protested.

How do you respond to the idea that unions should not limit themselves to one party, but caucus in them all?

That is an interesting model that gives points of influence and of entry into parties. We have noticed something particular with the current Trade Union Bill that is going through parliament, because we have spent much more time and effort talking to Tory MPs and Lords than on any previous occasion. We have noticed just how distant they are from our understanding of the situation; they knew very little about us and, to be honest, we didn't know very much about them.

So, there's a whole educational process going on.

An educational process *needs* to go on, although I can't say that we have managed to stop this Bill in its tracks. But the opening up of some channels of dialogue and exchange of views has been useful, because we have to show people that this is the worst Bill since the Tebbit Bill of 1982. The new legislation will remove the Wages Councils and thereby take away all minimum protection for about 2.5 million people who are not in well unionised areas. It impedes unions by complicating the 'check-off' system, which deducts union subscriptions from wages; it abolishes the TUC's ability to sanction on inter-union disputes; and makes industrial action extremely complicated with postal ballots, a week's notice, and the imposition of Citizen Charter type action which will allow individuals to take legal action against unions.

But it seems that the Tories may be going too far. The unions are now highly regarded, as current opinion polls are showing, and, as with the miners, people are saying, 'How much more can they take?' The unions have been weakened by years of hostile legislation and unemployment, but now there is a sort of sympathy vote.

Those views are around and are reflected in the opinion polls. But there is also a feeling around that we need the unions. This has grown because the alternative models, such as the Japanese one of guaranteeing job security in exchange for loyalty and commitment, are now very rocky. In Japan companies that made such promises are laying people off, as are companies like IBM. And firms like Marks and Spencer have refused to honour some offers of jobs to graduates. Companies that have been associated with non-union policies and with success are no longer looking so successful.

How will the 'super unions' fit into this? Will the big, amalgamated, sectoral unions be more effective in dealing with the new situation? This could, in fact, be a challenge to the TUC. It has been said that if there were just three super unions then the TUC would have no role, but if there were six such unions, then there would be a role for the TUC. Are not some of these amalgamations 'political' and therefore rather artificial; and are some of them suffering from 'amalgamation indigestion' having swallowed so many other organisations? In this situation could the TUC find a new future role as a campaigning, coordinating body?

Union amalgamations are inevitable and the pace will, no doubt, accelerate. By the end of the century the TUC will probably drop from over 70 affiliates to less than 40. Within that there will be some large blocks and there will still be smaller, sectoral organisations. The super union problem for the TUC is overstated. For example the three largest unions in Germany account for 75 per cent of the DGB's membership, and we are a long way from that at the moment. The direction of union amalgamations is far from clear. The engineering/electrical amalgamation, AEEU, is a very important block in traditional manufacturing; while Unison, an amalgamation of Nupe, Nalgo and Cohse, is important across the public sector. But the key question that the TUC stands or falls by is the quality of relationships between those unions, and their ability to act together on the big issues of the day. If they could act together without any intermediary that would be fine, but nobody in those unions would seriously argue that case. We need a strong united voice on employment, economics, labour law, social justice and fairness, and on campaigning for support for trade union goals. And that will be the TUC's role whether there are three, 33 or 333.

PART TWO

THINGS OLD, NEW, BORROWED AND GREEN:
ECONOMICS IN THE 1990s

THREE-THIRDS BRITAIN

Will Hutton interviewed by Mike Power

Mike Power: Before coming directly on to questions of full employment and what you think the trade union movement can do about them, let us talk about your recent, very interesting writings about the casualisation of labour and its social consequences. Would you describe modern casualisation and explain its nature?

Will Hutton: This is an idea that is still in its early stages. It is useful to think about Britain's labour force falling into three essential categories, which I describe as the 'third-third-third society'. Everyone will recognise the bottom, or marginalised, third. It includes the 10 per cent of the adult population who are out of work, and another 20 per cent who are working for 60 per cent of median wages (approximately £135 per week). There is another 4 to 5 per cent of the adult population who want to get into the labour market. These people are poor in relation to the average, and in some cases absolutely poor, because they are not eating properly and cannot clothe and feed their children properly. Such marginalised people are not easy to organise, and many of them see little point in voting.

The next third is the 'newly insecure'. When I first considered this section I thought of referring to them as the 'newly commoditised' but I felt that too few people would understand. However casualisation is, in an absolute sense, turning labour into a commodity, as it would be understood in a Marxist category; and this can happen across the income scale. For example, people who are earning three times the average wage can be on short-term contracts, which can cease. These are people at the upper end of income distribution. Those at the lower end of the scale consider those at the top to be in a 'less bad' position, which is true, but those top-enders have big mortgages and nevertheless feel themselves to be profoundly insecure.

This 'newly insecure' third have very good reason to feel like that don't they?

Yes, this is a fast growing section of the working population. Some 17 per cent of the workforce fell out of collective bargaining agreements between 1984 and 1990, when just 51 per cent remained covered. Unionisation of the employed labour force declined during the 1980s from around 55 per cent in 1979 to under 40 per cent today. People are now having to make their own provisions for pensions, holiday pay, sickness and paternity or maternity leave. However, the growth in casualisation is being driven partly by demand. Such demand comes, for instance, from women whose husbands are in secure employment, or from people with large savings. These people are prepared to work at irregular times, but they are a minority. So there is a demand, but this should not be overstated, because what is really happening is on the supply side. For example, British Airways (BA) wants its full time employees to go part time, and is offering a bonus incentive. BA will benefit in three ways from this. Firstly, it will have people available when planes arrive and employ them for that specific time. Secondly, it gets flexibility in managing its costs, because if air traffic falls away they can simply lay people off, or not renew short-term contracts. Thirdly, if people work for less than 16 hours per week they are not eligible for the national insurance scheme, and even if they work more than 16 hours the sickness, health and pension benefits that come with full time employment are absolved. They save on social overheads and have a more flexible workforce, which can meet the ebbs and flows of daily business, and of the economic cycle. Risk is therefore being displaced onto the labour force. This phenomena is happening in every industry and it is having a big impact on the economy at large.

Your third, 'third' is, no doubt, those in secure jobs, but how secure are they?

The last third are those in full time, pensionable employment, and who are covered by collective bargaining agreements. This used to be the 'norm', but even this third now have their pay linked more closely to the rhythm of the economy, through bonuses and profit-sharing schemes. Such schemes, which covered around 15 per cent in the early 1980s, have increased to include nearly half today. Employers in this category are paying less in basic pay with the rest of the wage being profit related. This element of the labour force is slightly more secure, because when times get hard wages are cut rather than jobs. Therefore although they feel themselves to be increasingly at risk this is a privileged 'third'. Now with mortgage rates at a 25 year low, they are beginning to buy houses, and holidays and some consumer goods – they will be the driving force of any economic recovery. But they cannot drive very far because, in the housing market for example, there cannot be an improvement without the 'house price ladder' working. And the ladder, or chain, extends into the next third. Even the bottom, most marginalised third, are potential players in the housing market, as renting is no longer an easy option.

The social and economic consequences of your description are enormous. According to your model, insecurity now ranges across all social classes, and this is having a debilitating effect on people's confidence. Is the big economic consequence the end of the consumer society?

In macroeconomic terms the consumer society is now behind us as people no longer feel optimistic that tomorrow will be better than today. They no longer feel that if they take on a big commitment their income will be secure enough to allow them to service large debts. Therefore, the belief that a consumption-led economic recovery is under way is misleading. Mass producers need a mass consumption market, but such a market is disappearing with the creation of this 'third-third-third' society. Economists, at the end of the nineteenth and in the early twentieth centuries, observed that it is economically inefficient to have acute inequalities in income. They believed this because if purchasing power is concentrated among the rich and super rich, or in my model among the secure or advantaged, they do not, on their own, have the purchasing power to sustain production or a recovery. This situation will lead to a renewal of inflation, because the government will have to hold interest rates down for longer than it will wish in order to get a recovery going.

And remember that what looks like a recovery now is only an

upward oscillation around a declining rate of economic growth in Britain. In 1979 economic growth was 3 per cent a year, now it is just over 2 per cent and will fall again to 1.5 per cent if policies do not change. These oscillations will undoubtedly get more violent; having gone below trend in recent years we are now moving in the other direction. This will be mistaken for a recovery by the Conservative press and their legions of propagandists. But this is merely an upward oscillation around a declining trend. The important thing however is to keep watching what is happening in the fundamental structures of the economy.

Those are some of the economic consequences, but the social effects of the 'third-third-third' society are also acute. They can be seen geographically. The one third of newly insecure, for example, are living between the inner and outer suburbs of the big cities. This 'third' which used to sustain those 'three up, three down' semi-detached houses and all the economic life around them, like the local shops, are less able to do so now. By contrast the outer suburbs remain relatively prosperous and the gentrified inner sub-urbs are still doing quite well. But there are huge areas of the inner cities where the marginalised live that are visibly run down. There is a clear geographic ghettoisation corresponding to people's incomes, sense of security and job expectations. This is having all sorts of effects on social provisions like education, because those in the top third who can afford to opt out tend to do so. Consequently the pool of people in the state system come from distressed families, and the behaviour and performance of schools in their areas is worse than those in the advantaged areas. As the levels of crime, particularly in the marginalised areas, are now quite shocking, it is impossible to escape the disintegration of Britain's social structure. The most invidious aspect of all this is that the advantaged choose to opt out of a universal system, but such a system that caters for the other two thirds, is now populat-ed by people on low incomes, who are under stress and are 'hold-ing back the children of the advantaged'. This is creating a kind of social apartheid between the 'three thirds' which is driven by the social phenomena around it and the value system above it.

What can the trades unions do in this situation that is new and different? The unions grew in the post-war era of full employment, nationalisation and welfarism, and were partly the architects of

that settlement. Today, however, they seem to have lost their role in a post-Fordist era of mass unemployment and privatisation. Do you think it possible for the unions to intervene within the world of work, in this new situation, and create for themselves the kind of moral authority that will help to rebuild their membership base and relevance?

There are a number of important issues here. First, there is a battle of ideas to be won. Socialism was a very powerful idea at the beginning of this century, its opposition to the world of markets and exploitation gave people direction, and was immediately understood. Part of the unions' helplessness at the moment is the lack of such an idea about organising society in a different way. But now there are many ideas around that can be used towards constructing a new model of the way we live, and could animate a non conservative party of the left. Secondly, the unions could encourage the Labour Party into a new political strategy. It may be true that Labour could win the next General Election in a first-past-the-post contest, but then it would take control of the parliamentary system and state, which is a fundamental conservative construct. That system and state is anti pluralist, anti universalist and is hostile to Labour's aims. Therefore it is impossible to 'win' on a first-past-the-post basis and make fundamental changes, because if you want a pluralist society you cannot 'win' by not embracing pluralism in your victory.

Labour has to rethink its own constitution and Jack Straw is right about the need to replace Clause Four. Labour needs a new statement of aims, which the unions should help to construct – in addition both the party and unions need to democratise themselves. Such a process should include an electoral pact with the Liberal Democrats. One of the constituent and binding elements of such a hegemonic alliance, which the Labour Party would be at the centre of, would be the unions, alongside northern manufacturers, some small business people, and those in the English regions and Scotland and Wales. This could form a powerful non conservative, counter-hegemonic, coalition. The unions should be encouraging Labour in this direction. The alliance needed to confront conservative hegemony has to be much more broad-based than that on which the labour movement was founded. To be sufficiently broad that alliance has to respect its constituent elements.

It has to give them 'constitutional protection' from having their autonomy usurped.

How could these elements in such a coalition have their autonomy protected?

Well, for example, small business people, whose firms are a basic element of the British economy, will have to be reassured that they will not be nationalised, or regulated out of existence. However, they will also have to accept that the constitutions of their firms will be reshaped so that other stakeholders, apart from the owners of the enterprise and its immediate managers, should have a direct say in the running of firms. These are, after all, human organisations. This reconstituting of the firm would change the landscape of British capitalism. But even with big potential changes ahead small business people would know that when they are part of, and vote for, a non conservative coalition, they will ultimately be better off. They will be better off because business would be stimulated and they would benefit, and because the society in which they operate their businesses will be much healthier. Therefore, although they will be circumscribed in their actions and will be behaving differently, they could see that they will be independent and able to pursue their business instincts, which is ultimately to make money.

How would you present the case to political people?

When I talk to Liberal Democrat audiences I always talk about realignment, proportional representation and constitutional reform. When I talk to a Labour audience I always talk about Gramsci and the war of manoeuvre and hegemonies. On the ground they both mean the same thing which is about electoral pacts, joint programmes, and establishing political pluralism. The unions have to signal to the Prescotts, the Kaufmans and the Hattersleys, who I respect as long-standing fighters for social justice, that they are unwillingly, or unintendedly, handmaidens of British conservatism, because Labour keeps entering elections with no prospect of winning and thereby legitimises the conservative state. Regarding the unions, they should think of themselves more as professional organisations. With this in mind the nurses and caring unions have done very well by stressing their professionalism, rather than as workers against organised capital. Unions should also take a more active role in things like managing pensions, but there is a dilemma here because until there is a change of regime they are unlikely to be pulled into the system. However I feel very bullish about the unions, as I am a believer in buying at the bottom and selling at the top, whether in the stock market, the housing market or in political ideas and the unions have been a long time in a bear market. Now, with the growth in insecurity, the unions have a really rich moment in which to recruit.

You suggest that unions should professionalise and continue to have a political role. But does this have to be a party political role even though the unions' political campaigning could benefit Labour? Do you think therefore that the unions and Labour Party should become unhinged?

Yes, and the language of the unions has to become much more universal. This is partly about style. During the recent railworkers strikes they failed to get the issue of insecurity across, which was the element in their case with which most people could have identified. Instead we saw Jimmy Knapp standing before an inscription in his office stating 'Unity is strength' and saying 'My members won't stand for it any more.' But the railworkers' case could have been linked to the wider world of job insecurity. The government and British Rail are imposing an incredible and unjustified level of insecurity on railworkers, but trains will continue to run, signals will be operated, and construction and maintenance undertaken. Railworkers missed an opportunity to make a link between what is happening in their industry to what is happening in every industry in Britain. Without that link being made commuters did not sympathise with the reasons for their journeys being disrupted. In the current era, with socialist ideas being so discredited, the unions need to be free to create a new body of ideas that will validate their actions. It speaks to nobody today to say that a strike is valid because 'organised Labour is striking against organised capital'. The unions need a new body of ideas from which slogans that are relevant to the 1990s can be drawn. These ideas have to be universalist and state that 'we all opt in'.

What is Wrong with Britain's Economy?

William Keegan interviewed by Stuart Wilks

THE ECONOMIC ESTIMATES for 1993/4 do not read well –
unemployment: 3.25 million; projected budget deficit: £50,000
million; balance of payments deficit: £17,500 million; economic
growth: 1.25 per cent. One does not need to be an economist to
realise that the problem here is that the first three numbers are
very big and the last number is very small. Moreover, one does not
even need to be an economist to seek to interpret them. Are current economic problems, as the government suggests, merely a
result of the severity of global recession in the 1990s? Or are the
economic indicators symptoms of a much deeper malaise, a deep-
rooted, structural problem in the British economy exacerbated by
the experience of Thatcherism, with its inherent dislike of manufacturing industry and in-built distrust of the public sector? I leave
the choice to you.

The economy is in bad shape, but so too is economic policy.
The government drifts directionless aboard Major's lifeboat, having bailed out of the sinking ship of monetarism. The government
blames the stormy sea for its lack of direction, but I cannot help
but wonder if the choice of craft is not the problem – lifeboats
have never been known to be particularly easy to steer. There is
seemingly no strategy, but even more worrying, the government
seems to lack the most basic policy goals. An economic policy void
like this has not been known since the 1930s, and at least then
there were serious alternative ideas. John Maynard Keynes'
General Theory offered a way in which the state could seek to
manage capitalism. Interestingly, advocacy of Keynesian techniques appears to be enjoying a steady revival and Christopher

Huhne of the *Independent* more or less accused Norman Lamont of being a closet Keynesian following his budget on 16 March 1993. Lamont may or may not be helping to bring Keynes back into fashion but there are a few economists, including Keegan, who never renounced Keynesianism.

Stuart Wilks: Is it not true that the economic policies of the 1980s are largely to blame for the budget deficit? In particular, the squandering of North Sea oil and the cutting of direct taxation subsidised through privatisation receipts?

William Keegan: Absolutely. The tax base was eroded in the 1980s. The buoyancy of revenue and the size of the tax base was falsified and people were misled by the combination of temporary selling of North Sea receipts and the very high rate of privatisation. Furthermore, the damage to the industrial base in the 1980s, when according to a House of Lords select committee, we lost between a fifth and a quarter of our industrial base, had a serious impact on the possibility of future tax revenues. So, there is a structural element to both the fiscal and the balance of payments problem. That suggests caution. It also points to the need for some imagination. It can be argued that the damage done to the country's long-term growth potential by the policies of the 1980s calls for a serious recovery effort and some imaginative schemes. So just waiting for an ordinary recovery to occur would not deal with the budget deficit entirely.

To pick up on the balance of payments – the fall in the value of North Sea oil revenues has made it clear that Britain's strength in invisible exports (insurance, banking, financial services) cannot cover the deficit incurred by Britain's decline in manufacturing exports. Is the only solution to the balance of payments problem therefore to rebuild Britain's manufacturing base?

One of the main tragedies of the 1980s was that people were fooled into thinking that wonderful things were happening to business when they were not. So, the long-term solution to Britain's balance of payments problem is to rebuild the manufacturing base. Obviously, this is a country which is not particularly given to planning in the way that some other countries are but the macroeconomic approach of a more competitive exchange rate and lower interest rates is certainly a start, however reluctant. The strategy has to be export-led. If industry sees the prospect, then the investment would take place in exports and import savings. This would take five to ten years which means, given the extraordinary fact that manufacturing imports rose by 6 per cent last year during the depths of recession and the vast balance of payments deficit, we cannot rely on an old-fashioned consumer boom to lead us out. It has to be a gentle recovery.

So there has to be a long-term plan?

Yes, there has to be a sense of strategy, and having a Department of Trade and Industry where the president of the Board of Trade is not consulted about interest rate changes is just laughable. This government is living from day to day. It may not believe in a Ministry of Planning, and the collapse of communism may have discredited continental European planning to some extent, but it is absurd to have no strategy for industry and these people have not got a strategy.

Compared to the 1930s, for example, we now have a much more structured international economic community, particularly within Europe, which offers more stability. It does seem that a recovery will have to come as a result of cooperation at the European level, which challenges traditional Keynesian policies. As a Keynesian, at what institutional level do you think economic policy should be determined?

Keynesianism in one country is difficult at a time like this and I favour what I hope is a cross-party belief that recovery requires a sort of Keynesian approach at the EC level. In the present situation, each country is living in fear of the other. You could introduce some coordinated expansion. This was talked about at the Edinburgh summit, but the figures involved were pretty small. They have also been thinking about infrastructure projects. Mr Delors realises the importance of this. But the British have just dragged their feet and the kind of problems that have affected our attitude to public sector projects also affect our coordination within Europe.

However much I agree with your perspective on economic policy, so much of it would represent a complete reversal of Tory policy that it seems we need a change of government to bring in these policies and enable European cooperation.

It is a tremendous disappointment that although the Conservative government changed its leader and there was this initial publicity about John Major and a classless society, he is a phenomenal failure when it comes to economic vision. Many people feel they were cheated at the last election. There is a need either for a change of government or for a change of leadership in the present government. Clearly, Michael Heseltine has been a bitter disappointment because people thought he would show some initiative at the Board of Trade and then he dealt himself a potentially mortal blow with the way that he handled the miners. So it does not look as if an economic vision is coming from Major or him and it's certainly not coming from the Chancellor. John Major performed a conjuring trick in terms of convincing people that things were going to be new and different, whereas they are not terribly, although they are in odd detail. But the Conservative Party in parliament is absolutely full of people who came up during the Thatcher era and it is appalling that the man now tipped to be Chancellor and possibly a new leader is Michael Portillo, an absolute dyed-in-the-wool Thatcherite and the last person we need to run the Treasury or the country.

As you discuss in your book, *The Spectre of Capitalism* **(London: Hutchinson, 1992) the belief that capitalism has succeeded and communism has failed has deep repercussions in that it has created an almost obsessive belief in markets. What should be the relationship between the market and the state?**

It is unfortunate that there is this extraordinary coincidence of the collapse of communism with this loss of nerve by capitalism. It was meant to be capitalism's finest hour but capitalism is all over the place. There is a re-run of the debates of the 1930s, with people worried about protectionism and scared of Taiwan and China. One of the things I cover in some detail in my book is that, unfortunately, the collapse of communism was, at least while Reagan and Thatcher were still there, associated with the triumph of extreme market economics, whereas what works best is an appropriate mixture of public and private sector. It is madness to have wholesale privatisation in Eastern Europe because these things should be done gradually. Clearly, successful private companies need a good public sector infrastructure. If the private sector can contribute to that infrastructure in ways that can reduce the Public

Spending Borrowing Requirement then fine, but in the end government's central role is to look at the wider interest both in the construction of infrastructure and in the regulation of the private sector.

BUILDING A GREEN AND MORE SUSTAINABLE SOCIETY

Michael Jacobs interviewed by **Quentin Given**

Quentin Given: Speaking as an economist, how far do we have to change our way of life to make it sustainable?

Michael Jacobs: In the short term some of the changes can be achieved through technological advances without much of an impact on people's lifestyles. For example, if industry can produce products using so called 'clean technology' which is now technically possible if not always commercially viable, there may be little change in the products we buy, but the environmental impact of producing them will be greatly reduced. Similarly, energy efficiency can be greatly improved through purely technical processes such as insulation, combined heat and power generation and improved controls on heating systems. However, undoubtedly at some point changes in lifestyles will be needed. The one that will have the greatest effect is restriction on the use of the private motor car. I do not see how this can be avoided. Investment in public transport and changes and land use to make things more accessible can do a lot to minimise the painful effects, but this is still going to be the most difficult change we're going to have to face over the next 15 to 20 years.

Over what timescale are these changes needed?

We have to start now. Many of the most urgent problems are with us already – deforestation and desertification in the south, air and water pollution in the industrialised countries, loss of habitat and countryside and so on. These need immediate attention. But even the longer term issues like global warming require immediate action because of time lags. Global temperature increases in 30 years' time will arise because of current carbon dioxide emissions. Ozone depletion will get worse for many years because of past and present CFC emissions. So starting now is really already too late. Lifestyle changes, however, need to be gradual. People have to understand why change is needed and they have to be able to see the benefits of change. If not, there won't be consent. And if there isn't consent, ultimately policies will be rejected, and there won't be change.

What kind of policies will we need?

First, we will need continued, and strengthened, regulation. To raise pollution standards, to improve energy efficiency in buildings, to prevent destruction of natural habitats, etc, we'll need to tighten environmental and planning laws. In many cases we may be able to build financial incentives into regulatory measures. It's a mistake to think that using the law and using so called 'market mechanisms' (like green taxes and subsidies) are opposed to one another. They're complementary. So, for example, we might impose a charge on landfilled waste as well as laws to reduce packaging. We might provide lower stamp duty on purchases of more energy efficient houses, as well as stricter insulation standards. And so on.

Second, we will need to supplement these regulatory measures with hands-on industrial policies. Like the Japanese, Germans and Swedes, governments will need to assist key sectors to meet environmental targets by providing research and development grants and loans for the introduction of cleaner and more efficient technologies. New 'environmental' sectors will need specific support, even direct investment. They may require the establishment of a new national investment bank, since the financial markets are so notoriously short-term in their approach and environmental investments are likely to show long-term benefit.

Third, I believe we will need to shift the basis of taxation. At the moment we have low or zero taxes on energy resources, wastes and pollution – the environmental 'bads' we wish to reduce. And we have relatively high taxes on labour, saving and value added, which are 'goods' we wish to increase. If we could begin to shift taxes from 'goods' to 'bads' we would provide a general incentive to cut the bads – that is, reduce environmental damage – and to increase the goods, particularly employment. Such a change would need to be gradual, to minimise transitional costs, but in economic and environmental terms it would be clearly beneficial. As a way of raising tax revenues, by contrast with income taxes, it might also be rather politically attractive. I wouldn't be surprised to see increasing interest in this idea over the next few years.

People tend to vote for short-term prosperity, and against tax increases. How can environmental policies be made palatable to the electorate?

This is partly a problem of articulation. Politicians are not very good at explaining how quality of life, that is, those things which society buys collectively or which are a 'free gift' of nature, contribute to peoples' standard of living. In political debate standard of living is reduced to the 'pound in your pocket', your post-tax disposable income. Most people would accept that a clean environment, clean air, clean water, a beautiful countryside, their own personal health, and some degree of security about the future, are components of their standard of living. But the debate is articulated in the narrow terms of disposable income. So first politicians and the media must articulate a notion of standard of living in a way that incorporates 'quality of life'.

Secondly, many people do not appreciate that if nothing is done, things will get much worse. They see a choice between environmental policies which they believe may make them worse off and carrying on living as they are now. But we cannot carry on living as we do. We need to show what it is going to be like if changes are not made.

People in the environmental movement talk about environmental policy safeguarding the interests of 'future generations'. This gives a grasp of timescales, but in a way it's unhelpful because the people we are talking about are not abstract people we do not know and can only have some altruistic concern for. They are our children and our grandchildren. If I have children in my mid-thirties, they won't have reached retirement age by the year 2050, when it is predicted global warming will become really severe. Their children, my grandchildren, will be alive in the year 2100. We can articulate environmental concerns in terms of people we will know, love, and care about, without any degree of altruism or abstract theorising.

Is there any prospect of the Labour or Conservative Parties being persuaded into adopting these policies?

I think we're entering a period comparable to the pre-war years when many industrialists realised that a welfare state and improved employment conditions could not only be lived with, but might actually be beneficial to capitalism. So now I think that many industrialists realise that environmental improvements not only need not be too costly, but can also improve productivity. Moreover, they are required to preserve a healthy workforce and decent quality of life – as well as global political stability. You can see this trend emerging in the statements and reports of organisations such as the (government established) Advisory Council on Business and the Environment, and the International Chamber of Commerce, which includes many of the largest multinational companies (and largest polluters). Of course, there will be resistance as well – as there was before the creation of the welfare state, with many industrialists opposing environmental improvements as they opposed (and continue to oppose) employment ones. But I think this trend will mean that all parties in the industrialised world will gradually 'go Green' over the next 10 to 15 years. Indeed, to a considerable extent this has already happened, even if only at the theoretical level – it's now unacceptable even for Tory Ministers to be anti-environmental in the way that was commonplace just a few years ago.

The question really is the pace of change. And here I think we have to emphasise the role of civil society outside the political parties. Certainly, in respect of the Labour Party, I don't really see the change coming from within. Or, rather, it will be the pressure from environmental organisations, community action and the general public concern which will give the Greens inside the Labour Party the influence to change policy. I am actually rather hopeful about this – I think there are distinct signs that the party is beginning to 'think green' in a way that's much more serious and profound than before. We'll see!

A handful of transnational companies are responsible for a large part of resource depletion and pollution around the world. How can we enforce these policies on these companies?

There is no substitute for international regulation. That is why the

EC is so important, for only on that scale can anything be done about transnational corporations. No transnational can avoid the European market as a whole in the way they can avoid locating in any individual country. While it is a long way from imposing the sort of environmental and social controls that would be ideal, the EC does have this potential. The critical advance needed is for the EC to introduce regulation in Europe relating to transnational companies' activities in the Third World.

What are the implications of a Green economic and energy strategy for the coal industry?

This is a good example why environmentalists cannot divorce themselves from the 'old' politics of left and right, as some Greens have supposed. Environmental objectives must be harnessed to social ones concerned with the distribution of income and power in society. There are different ways of protecting the environment: some are more egalitarian in terms of power and resources, others are less so.

It is quite wrong to destroy the coal industry in the way the government has done. Most environmentalists argue that coal is an important part of British energy policy for security of supply reasons, and that de-sulphurisation equipment should be installed to make coal less damaging to the environment. In the longer term there will have to be a decline in the use of coal, as there will be for all fossil fuels because of carbon dioxide emissions and the greenhouse effect, but this will have to be managed slowly to protect mining communities. A Green economic policy in Britain over the next twenty years will have to see a much higher emphasis on energy efficiency, and on investment in renewable sources.

The 'dash for gas', which is the main threat to the coal industry, is environmentally stupid. Producing electricity from burning gas is a bad use of gas because it can be used much more efficiently to heat buildings directly. It is a reflection of Britain's environmentally weak regulation of the energy industry, which encourages the industry to build more power stations rather than to conserve energy. Parts of the US and Canada have a system of 'least-cost planning' under which energy companies are not allowed to build new power stations if it is cheaper for them to conserve energy. So electricity supply companies give energy-efficient light bulbs and energy-efficient heating systems to households paid for out of reduced bills because that is cheaper than building new power stations. That is the sort of regulation needed here. The 'dash for gas' goes entirely against it and it is mining communities which are paying the price.

Do you think Lamont's budget really represents the beginnings of a 'greening' of fiscal policy?

No. This is a cynical ploy on the government's part to cloak a revenue raising measure in Green rhetoric. First, no one believes they are committed to environmental reform of the tax system in any other way. Second, the impact on global warming will be minimal. There will be some cut in carbon dioxide emissions, but it will not be very great because people do not cut their energy consumption much in response to price changes. Those that do are the very poorest who cannot afford the extra amount on their bills, and therefore just go without. Fuel poverty in Britain is a national scandal: many pensioners and other poor people already experience what is called 'home shrinkage': their home is reduced to the one room that they can afford to heat. This sort of saving in domestic energy is not a major contribution to reducing global warming emissions and has terrible social consequences. What is needed are measures to enable people to cut their energy consumption without cutting the warmth of their homes through insulation, efficient heating systems and so on. A national energy efficiency programme would do far more to cut carbon dioxide emissions and could create thousands of jobs. Moreover, it could pay for itself through lower energy bills. If we had such a programme, then I think we could tax energy. The price of energy doesn't reflect its environmental costs, and a higher price would provide an incentive to use it more efficiently. But the tax should be levied not at the consumption end, as VAT, but at the production end, as a carbon (and nuclear) tax, to encourage investment in renewable and to provide incentives for industrial and transport efficiency improvements.

Pursuing the issue of poverty, what does the largely middle class Green movement have to offer the poor of our society?

First, many environmental policies will benefit poorer people more than the rich. For example, cleaning up air quality and improving public transport will benefit the elderly, women and children who do not have access to cars, and poorer people who live in neighbourhoods with the most polluted air.

Second, there is evidence that environmental protection overall will create employment. This is because improving environmental efficiency generally requires investment in new plant and equipment, which created jobs. For example, installing insulation and energy efficient heating systems in housing could generate 165,000 jobs over a 10 year period.

Third, on the specific issue of energy, environmental protection ought to cut poorer people's bills. Last, the critical issue for everyone is how people understand the 'standard of living'. As environmental policies come into force, lifestyles will change. But whether standards of living fall or rise is a matter of subjective interpretation – whether people feel the changes make them better or worse off. And the environmental movement can influence the way changes are perceived. Using the car less, for example, may not be perceived as a loss if people find they can walk to where they need to go, if public transport is improved or if people do not need the car so much because they live closer to their work and other services When people find the streets are not so congested, the air quality is better and it takes less time to get to their destination, they may feel this is actually an improvement in their standard of living.

Change will happen. But the subjective experience of change can be influenced and this is what we need to be working for. We can create a society which values a healthy, beautiful and stable environment – a green society, if you like.

IT DOES NOT HAVE TO BE LIKE THIS

Frank Blackaby

BRITISH SOCIETY IS in a wretched state. We have misery on a scale not seen for 60 years. Not since the 1930s has there been such a universal air of depression, such a fear of poverty, such an absence of hope. Contrast it with the early post-war years, when – in spite of all the problems of rationing and shortages – Sam Watson, leader of the Durham miners, could say, 'Poverty has been abolished. Hunger is unknown. The sick are tended. The old folk are cherished. Our children are growing up in a land of opportunity.' A land of opportunity now? The standard economic commentators – who tend to live in stockbrokers' offices these days – have nothing for our comfort. There are widespread forecasts that unemployment will stay around three million until the end of the century. Very few forecasters are willing to hazard the hope that the number will come down below two million. The budget does nothing to change these forecasts. Unemployment is still more likely to rise than to fall this year. Next year and the year after, the scheduled tax increases will help to keep unemployment high. The specific measures in the budget for the long-term unemployed are minuscule.

This is all wrong. We can go back to full employment. Unemployment could be made to fall as fast as it rose over the last three years, beginning from next month. We had full employment in this country for just over 25 years, and we could have it again. What has been done, can be undone. I recall making this point in my last exchange with the present permanent secretary to the Treasury a long time ago. His reply, which I thought and still think was somewhat lame, was: 'You can't say that.'

It is curious that there is so little folk memory of those years of full employment, and it is puzzling too that people have so easily been fooled into believing that unemployment is some act of God, beyond political control. There is a great deal of re-education to be done – to persuade politicians that managing the economy is not the same as running a grocery shop in Grantham. To that end, this article does three things. Firstly, it presents some necessary kindergarten economics: necessary, because current discussion has lost sight of the big arguments. Secondly, it tries to clear out of the way some of the intellectual lumber which clogs up thinking about unemployment. After that it discusses policy. Finally, how can a government, which believes that it can get away with three million unemployed, be persuaded to act? We need to find ways of empowering the poor, the unemployed, the dispossessed.

Kindergarten economics

The central economic problem is production – to produce enough for a reasonable standard of living for the inhabitants of any state, or group of states. Through most of recorded history, resources were too limited for that to be possible – and it is still not possible in most of the world. But in the western industrial world, the problem of adequate productive capacity has been solved – and solved a long time ago. The western industrial states can, with difficulty, produce enough for an adequate standard of living for all their inhabitants.

It is, of course, the rise in productivity, in output-per-person which over the long term has produced this potential prosperity, and which can continue to do so if managed sensibly. Each year it takes 2-3 per cent less labour input to produce last year's output of goods and services. Fewer people are needed to run the telephone system; fewer bank clerks to run the banks. The economy should be managed so that this is a bonus, and not a tragedy. The bonus can be taken either as an increase in output of other goods and services – including government provided services – or as increased leisure. Over the long period of full employment, the division was roughly two-thirds to increased output, one-third to increased leisure. What is stupid is to run the economy in such a way that rising productivity produces increased misery instead of increased satisfaction. That is what we are doing now. There is another example of this folly, in the class of goods labelled in national accounts as 'regrettable necessities'. Military expenditure is a regrettable necessity. We do not want tanks for their own sake; we only want them for security. If, because we have lost our enemies, we need fewer tanks, that is (or should be) a gain, not a loss. Once more, in the full employment period, it was a gain. In the four years after the Korean war, military spending in Britain was cut by one-third in real terms, and nobody noticed: unemployment at the end of four years was lower than it had been at the beginning. Full employment makes industrial transition much less painful; in periods of full employment, about one-third of those employed in manufacturing industry change their jobs in any case each year.

It is stupid to run the economy in such a way that nine-tenths of those who want to work have long hours, and one-tenth have nothing to do. Again, this is kindergarten stuff. Ask any six-year-old this question: there are two men, and there is a ditch to be dug. One man can take 48 hours, while the other man stands by and does nothing. Or the two men can dig it, each working 24 hours. Which is better?

These elementary points are necessary: they have been lost in current discussion. In the western world, we can without any difficulty produce enough for a good standard of living for all. Secondly, we could arrange the labour input so that it was shared among those who wanted to work. These are simply matters of sensible economic arrangement.

Intellectual lumber

The 1990s are proving to be as bad as the 1930s in shoddy thinking about economic policy. There is a great deal of intellectual lumber to be cleared out of the way. For example, it is commonly said that the objective of an economy is to produce wealth. It is not. The objective of an economy is to produce welfare – that is, a flow of satisfactions. The provision of work for those wanting to work is a very important part of that flow. Economic theory has never been good at coping with the fact that most people of working age want a job – that work is a plus, not a minus. The UN Convention on Human Rights includes among those rights, the right to work – and so it should.

The doctrine which has dominated this government's economic policy says the market economy is self-regulating – or, alternatively, self-regulating with a simple rule. This is an extraordinary belief – that a system as complex as a modern industrial economy should be self-regulating with a simple rule. To anyone with any understanding of the behaviour of complex systems, it is about as likely as a monkey producing a sonnet on a typewriter. The origin of this curious view, incidentally, goes back to the Victorians and their devout belief in Providence. True, the nature of the simple rule kept changing: various measures of the quantity of money, the medium-term financial strategy, and so on. The latest version is the belief that, once inflation is brought down, economic growth will automatically resume. How long ago was it that we first heard that 'everything was in place' for economic recovery? A market economy is not in any sense self-regulating. It can spiral down into a quite unnecessary recession, and it can, if there is no correction, run with very high levels of unemployment.

All Conservative chancellors have repeated the dictum: 'We cannot spend our way out of a recession.' The exact opposite is true. There is no way that output can rise unless some category of real expenditure also rises: that is a simple statistical fact. Real output and real expenditure are two sides of the same coin – by definition identical. It can be any category of expenditure – consumer demand, investment demand, net exports or government expenditure. Government expenditure is just as good as any other – on some occasions better, because there is less immediate leakage into imports. The correct statement is this: for output to rise, real expenditure has to rise. The government should act to make sure that this happens.

Another standard axiom of this administration is that government spending cannot create real jobs. I suggest that Major, Lamont and Shephard do a tour of hospital casualty departments, to tell the doctors and nurses on duty that they are not doing real jobs. They can then proceed to Bosnia to inform the soldiers in the Cheshire regiment that their jobs, too, are unreal. This government speaks of world recession as if it was an act of God, like earthquakes and hurricanes. Perhaps the Prime Minister should ask the Archbishop of Canterbury to check with God whether He is angry with the western industrial world. Recessions are man-made, and with sensible economic policies they can be avoided. We do need, as Delors has suggested, collective action now in Europe; unfortunately many of the politicians in the other EC countries are as benighted as our own. Certainly it is more difficult than it used to be for one country alone in the EC to adopt a full employment policy: but it can be done. The British government should encourage collective action – it failed to do so when it had the EC presidency. It should inform its EC partners that it will put forward expenditure proposals in the EC which will bring western Europe back to full employment; however, if the other EC countries are unwilling, then Britain will follow a full employment policy on its own.

One of the more abysmal ideas around at the moment is the idea of handing over economic policy to central bankers. Central bankers are 'one objective' men. They want to bring inflation down and keep it down, and believe that there is nothing else that economic policy can do. If central bankers were given charge of economic policy in Europe, we would probably have 10 per cent unemployment forever. We have the constant Conservative assertion that there is no connection between rising unemployment and crime. It beggars belief that the Conservative Party politicians can still go on saying this. We live in an acquisitive society. It is obvious that the 16-20 year olds who cannot get jobs will be tempted to try to get money or goods in some other way. Crime is easy, and not many thieves get caught. The standard Conservative comment is that many unemployed people do not commit crimes: and that it exonerates the criminal to refer to any connection between unemployment and crime. Of course it does no such thing. The social cost of unemployment, not just in increased crime, but also in bad health and broken families, is very high. The direst cost estimate of £27,000 million, around £9,000 for each unemployed person, is much too low. Including the social costs, the figure is probably closer to £12,000.

In the argument over the social chapter, the government insists that reducing hours of work would increase unemployment. Refer back here to kindergarten economics – to the obvious silliness of an arrangement where nine people out of ten work long hours and one out of ten does no work at all. The idea is not that Britain alone should reduce the length of the working year, but that EC states should collectively agree to do so; then no state would be left with a competitive advantage. It is quite clearly time to take some of the gain from increased productivity in paid leisure. It may well be time to move to a four-day week in the western industrial world. There is also currently the belief that unemployment can be solved by more training; teaching school-leavers to write good letters of application, and so on. More training is not enough; the jobs are not there – not for the skilled either. At any time, the total number of jobs available is fixed by the total demand for labour in the economy, so increasing the supply of trained workers will do nothing to increase total employment.

It is this government's belief that it can do something about inflation, but nothing about employment, and that the only instrument which can be used is the rate of interest. Wrong. The rate of interest is a rather bad instrument of policy. When it is pushed up, it penalises the wrong people – small firms and house owners with mortgages. When it is pushed down, its reflationary effect is weak: it is like pushing on a piece of string. It is much better to use government expenditure or income.

We are frequently reminded that we are in an ageing society. Pensioners are living longer. Those of working age will have to support an increasing number of old people. This is true. A sensible policy would keep as many people in work as long as possible, so that the burden of supporting the pensioners is kept down. This is one more illustration of the folly of present policies. Over three million people are taken out from the 'work' side and put on the dependent side. Then there is talk of cutting pensions. This is not an exhaustive list of the economic follies of the present time. It may be enough to suggest that stockbrokers' economics has lost its way.

Policies

The policy needed for full employment is straightforward. The demand for labour is much too low, and it has to be increased. However the ideological economic brainwashing of the last decade and a half has been such that the Labour front bench – and the Liberal Democrats too – are terrified of the accusation of fiscal irresponsibility. They cannot free themselves from Granthamite economics.

History may help – in the early days of the New Deal in the USA, Roosevelt and the men round him were not socialists, and they had never heard of Keynes. They were just determined to get unemployment down. They persuaded Americans that it could be done. In the words of the historian of the New Deal, Arthur Schlesinger: 'By bringing to Washington a government determined to govern, Roosevelt unlocked new energies in a people who had lost faith, not just in government's ability to meet the economic crisis, but almost in the ability of anyone to do anything.' That describes precisely the loss of faith we have in Britain now. Consider the first winter of the New Deal. There was some delay in getting the Public Works Administration under way. In October 1933, Roosevelt gave Harry Hopkins the go-ahead to create new jobs that winter. On 15 November, Hopkins set up the Civil Works Administration (CWA) and announced his objective: 'The employment of four million by 15 December, 1933' – that is, within one month. He missed that target date – by 14 December there were only 2,610,451 on CWA rolls. But by mid-January – in two months flat – he was well over the four million mark.

The point is not the exact form of the New Deal's job creation – though some of the ideas, such as the Civilian Conservation Corps, could be used now with very little change. The point is rather that Roosevelt was absolutely determined to get unemployment down. Virtually all the pundits, then as now, said that it could not be done. He said it could, and he did it.

In Britain now the private sector is most unlikely, in aggregate, to create any significant number of new jobs until there is a general recovery in confidence. But there will be no general recovery in confidence so long as unemployment goes on rising, and more and more people begin to fear that they will lose their jobs as well. This is a Catch-22 situation. There is only one way out. The government will have to create jobs to stop unemployment from continuing to rise. Can it do this? Of course it can. The first thing it should do, if it wants to bring unemployment down, is to stop putting it up. It is at present busy forcing local authorities to reduce their labour force. As we know, this government hates local authorities because so many of them are Labour controlled. None the less the right thing to do now is for the government to swallow hard, increase employment in the health and education services, and ask local authorities to put forward schemes for employing, say, an additional 300,000 workers.

The money

The nature of the objection is known. We have seen it time and time again in interviews on unemployment. The interviewee puts forward some sensible ideas for creating employment. The Paxmans and Dimblebys of this world lean forward to deliver their killer punch: 'And where would you find the money?' I long for the day when someone, smiling a little and in a matter of fact voice replies: 'I would create it,' for that is the right answer.

Three questions. Can the government create money? Of course it can. The superior way of referring to the process is to call it 'underfunding'. The government issues short-term Treasury bills, the banks buy them and use them to increase their cash basis, so that they can create more credit. In this way the additional government borrowing does not lead to any shortage of credit, rather the contrary. Would this serve to increase the money supply? By most of the standard definitions of that elusive concept, it would. And an increase in the money supply at the moment is just what we need. Would this bring back domestically-driven inflation? It would not. Domestic inflation is driven by wage increases which exceed the rise in productivity. This is not going to be a problem for some years. It was the tragedy of this recession that the government could only think of one way of dealing with inflation – by creating massive unemployment. Then they found that the rise in unemployment got out of hand. Of course we have to find a better way of dealing with inflation, but that will be a problem for 1995, not 1993. The public sector borrowing requirement will go up further for a time: does that matter? It does not. At present both individuals and companies are in a saving mood, wanting to pay off debt. If a deeper recession is to be avoided, that money has to be spent by someone. In a recession such as the one we have now, only the government is likely to do this. The scale of government borrowing is only disturbing if it leads to excess demand and so to a high rate of inflation. That at the moment should be the least of the government's worries. Particularly in the housing sector now, we could do with gently rising prices.

What about the effect on the exchange rate of a move towards a full employment policy? It is unpredictable: it could go either way. One never knows what currency speculators will do – except that they will follow each other, up or down. In the US, a rise in output and a fall in unemployment has tended to strengthen the currency. In any case the objective of reducing unemployment is far more important than the objective of maintaining any particular exchange rate. It is not acceptable to try to use high unemployment as a way of dealing with the problem of inadequate export capability: indeed there is no reason to think it would be much help. Decrepit inner cities are hardly attractive sites for inward investment. If local authority employment schemes can make inner cities less decrepit, then a move towards full employment could in the long run benefit export capability.

In sum: it is time to stop the rise in unemployment and to start to bring it down – now, and not to rest on the hope that it might possibly stop rising in perhaps a year's time. Secondly, there is only one way to do anything about unemployment this year: the government must itself create the jobs. Thirdly, money itself is not the obstacle. The government can increase its borrowing and can underfund. The size of the borrowing requirement would be disturbing if there were a threat of domestically-generated inflation, or if government borrowing were to crowd out private investment. Neither development is on the present map of possibility.

Empowerment

This government believes – with some justification, given past experience – that unemployment does not lose elections. So it is not bothered that unemployment is generally forecast to rise all through this year. Each month we will have the usual statement of personal distress from the Employment Secretary, which we have heard now on over 30 occasions. We will be told, for the umpteenth time, that: 'There is no magic solution.' There may well be more fiddling of the figures to avoid big headline numbers. The Central Statistical Office will – as it has done in the past – try to maintain a series with consistent definitions, but that will not be the figure headlined each month in the media. The Labour Party will continue to put forward its rather timid programme: it is clearly nervous of appearing as the party of the poor and dispossessed, and doubts whether unemployment can be made into an election-winning issue. After all, the number of those in employment still far exceeds the number without work, and the government has had remarkable success in persuading the electorate that unemployment is not its fault. So there has been no categorical Labour Party statement that it would stop the rise in unemployment and bring it down to the full employment level of around 2-4 per cent.

It seems, then, that there is not much going for the unemployed. They have no powerful campaigning organisation. It would be hard to finance one, since by definition, they have no money to spare. Many of them doubt whether any party or organisation could do anything for them. None the less a campaigning organisation should be set up. It will need the support of those in work for its finance. What sort of things could it do? It should make a stir. Small meetings and small demonstrations are not much use. There has to be a big demonstration – of about one in ten of the unemployed and those who sympathise with them. That should bring out some 300,000 onto the streets. The demonstration could begin in Kennington Park, about 150 years after the great Chartist gatherings there. It is doubtful whether more pamphlets will help much. Somehow, ways have to found of bringing it home to this government that the present scale of unemployment is really unacceptable. For it does not have to be like this.

PART THREE

DEFENDING THE OLD, DEFINING THE NEW:

FORGING A NEW AGENDA FOR SOCIAL JUSTICE

BACK TO BEVERIDGE

Sir Gordon Borrie interviewed by **Kevin Davey**

Kevin Davey: When the Labour Party Commission on Social Justice was launched the *New Statesman* said that 'its chair, Sir Gordon Borrie, faces the Herculean task of spring cleaning the left-wing mind'. Is that an accurate description of your role?

Sir Gordon Borrie: I am not sure. Spring cleaning suggests that the mind of the left is in a terrible mess, when in fact there are some enduring values and ideas to build on. For example, the core concept of full employment remains central although it needs redefining to include flexible and part-time work, job sharing and so on. These are currently very important for women but, as time goes by, they will become important for men too. The left, insofar as it refuses to accept an indefinite residue of millions of people, who are abandoned to welfare cheques and non employment for long periods, understands the fundamental issue well.

You have described the commission as following in the footsteps of the Beveridge Committee. He identified five giants that had to be destroyed: disease, ignorance, want, squalor and idleness. Of these, he said idleness was the largest, the fiercest and the most important to attack. Every social security reform this committee recommended assumed that there would be full employment. Will that be true of the commission's report next year?

The economy has moved in a direction that Beveridge would not have approved of and our commission wants to get back to Beveridge. Let us leave aside for the moment the things that we know with hindsight he got wrong - the changes in the composition of poverty and the structure of families. These are things that Beveridge could not foresee. To get back to the truth of Beveridge means that there should be full and meaningful employment – not Work Fare or benefit plus £10 – and that cash benefits should be for temporary problems of sickness, unemployment or disablement. There may be some advantages in certain kinds of work in the public sector which are for the community or take place on a temporary basis, but these should not distract the commission from one of its central goals, which is to show how people can get real and meaningful jobs, that they are proud to talk about in the pubs, or to their friends, for example, and which give them dignity again. Of course some people are unable to work, for example, through disablement, and the elderly are not going to get young again. In these cases cash benefits will have to be permanent. But the majority of payments were always meant to be for people temporarily out of work.

This is no longer the case and the right does not seem to be particularly troubled by it. It has moved away from Beveridge's intention that benefits were not meant to be indefinite cash payments. There is a certain amount of disaffection with some aspects of the welfare state, but they are not particularly Beveridge's fault. They are because the government has gone back on the policies of full employment, and has failed to ensure that some of the Beveridge assumptions have continued. They have emphasised means testing for benefits and have not sought to combine economic policies with policies of social justice, as we intend to. For example, the government has failed to introduce child care on a big enough scale, and yet it would make economic sense as well as being socially just and in accordance with the current wishes of the electorate.

Can we afford the welfare state we need? Would it require the high tax and high spend government much of the electorate fears?

Naturally anyone on the left is conscious that a key question is always 'Where is the money coming from?', and a great deal of the answer is that mis-spent welfare will be redirected. It may be possible to target benefits without means testing. Certainly, it is wasteful to provide indefinite benefits to the long term unemployed and forfeit the lost tax revenue that would be available if they were provided with jobs. Long-term unemployment does not even have the Lamontian value of helping to fight inflation because the long term unemployed are not able to compete for jobs. To say nothing of all the other costs that disaffection and crime, insofar as they are related to unemployment, impose on the community. However, it is important to point out that on our regional visits – so far to Glasgow and Birmingham and Newcastle – we have discovered that communities are very active, even when they have inadequate or no resources to draw upon. Some self help and community projects are amazingly successful and if they were assisted by the government they could pay off, literally, in terms of real welfare. Much of it is a good deal better than the welfare coming out of the benefits agencies. We will make use of these sort of initiatives that are being discovered on the ground because they have not featured in the left's political discussion, much of which has been inspired by the ideas of the Webbs or Marx and regards the state as the provider of all good things. The commission is learning that there are many different ways of delivering welfare - through democratic agencies which work from the bottom up – which is not the same as a traditional local government administrative system.

Do the trade unions have any role in securing social justice? Are you concerned by their loss of rights and members, and the uncertainty over their future political role?

The role of trade unions is not very clear in all this, although it is important to support them. Historically they obviously have played a great role in securing social justice, although the industrial route and the political route have been traditionally two different, if complementary, ways whereby greater social justice was achieved. The future role of the trade unions is less certain. Trade unions are a big source of the information and views that we hope to get at. Margaret Wheeler, the General Secretary of COHSE is a member of the commission, and other members have trade union links.

Are the unions not essential to securing the wealth that you want to distribute more effectively? And are citizens not also entitled to social justice when they are at work? What would social justice for a miner look like in 1993?

This is difficult to answer. Miners are obviously an example of workers who have been extremely well organised in a trade union sense, despite the split. Unions like the NUM have a major role in arguing with government about closures and redundancies which affect the future of their industry. But their role will differ according to the level of unionisation of each industry. The disappearance of wages councils is also very troubling. For the low paid these were a substitute for trade union representation – although trade union support for individuals in their dealings with an employer have always been more effective than wages councils. Perhaps this is a vacuum which the trade unions should endeavour to fill. Certainly this issue gives rise to the sort of discussion which the commission needs to have, but is some way off yet, on the introduction of statutory minimum wages. Of course, individual workers still need assistance simply to articulate their case to the managers, or to make their case before an industrial tribunal, and trade union membership would be a way to get that. But if one goes down the route of greater governmental intervention to ensure minimum social justice by way of minimum wages, there could be a feeling on the part of trade unions that they are not so important. Yet there could also be an opportunity for unions to broaden their agenda beyond the bread and butter issues of wages and conditions of work to include flexible working, child care and democracy within the company.

It appears that one of Labour's biggest strategic problems has been sub-contracted to you: namely the question of how the party can retain the confidence of the relatively affluent tax payer and also deliver something of value to the poor. How far has the work of the commission progressed? How will it present its findings? And what impact do you think it will have?

I have thought a lot about this, because from the word go one wondered what it was all going to be for. The commission is very much at the beginning of its work and thus has come to no concrete decisions, so I have been giving you my personal views. They are informed, of course, by the discussions and visits that we have had. Some people in the Labour Party do not really care for the idea of a commission like this, independent or otherwise. They feel it means that MPs, members of the shadow cabinet and the National Executive, are not keeping a hold on the policy making machinery of the Labour Party. However, the commission is not a substitute for that. It is not even part of the policy making machinery of the Labour Party.

The commission has been set up by John Smith to look at the

issues and some long term objectives, just it may have been if John Smith was Prime Minister. The report will be presented to the Labour Party and simultaneously we will be presenting it to the world at large. Since it will be ready some time in the middle of Autumn 1994, and a General Election is not expected until 1996 or 1997, it is up to the policy making machinery of the Labour Party, including the conference the following year, to respond in its own way. We regard it as part of our role to try to forge a vision and to create objectives that make sense, not just for the immediate future, but on into the next century.

SOCIAL JUSTICE

David Donnison interviewed by **Willie Thompson**

Willie Thompson: Could you summarise for the readers of *New Times* the main lines of argument in your book *A Radical Agenda: After the New Right and the Old Left* (Rivers Oram: Rivers Oram Press, 1991)?

David Donnison: My aim is to renew a progressive standpoint by shedding the standard terms in which our political debate has been confined and asserting a radical view in words which anyone can understand. Progressives have always been concerned about human needs and about treating people in ways that give them self-respect. That means tackling the pain and exploitation which humiliate so many people. When large groups bear far more than their fair share of pain that is due to their powerlessness and involves poverty, public hostility and stigma. These basic injustices grow more urgent and scandalous as our country is increasingly divided. We are moving towards a 'two-thirds one-third' society, with the one third falling further and further behind the rest.

Some readers might feel that questions of anti-social behaviour – loan sharks, vandalism – should be more prominent in your discussion. Is it not true that such practices tend to be very prevalent in circumstances of poverty and deprivation?

If you work with people in areas where life is hard and many are either out of work or coping single-handed with children on low incomes, you find that crime, vandalism – more broadly, 'incivilities' – are high on their list of the things which must be put right. The people who live in these neighbourhoods are the main victims of such disorder: the vast majority are not responsible for it. They hate it and need to be given a chance of working together to establish better relationships. The response has to be a collective one, both in the sense of calling for civic leadership on a city-wide scale and in the sense of working with and supporting local initiatives. Left to themselves, people are compelled to adopt individual responses – buying big dogs, keeping steel shutters on their windows and staying off the street. These create a still more intimidating environment and make things worse. Civic leadership has been neglected in progressive thinking. Meanwhile, we have a central government which has actively set out to destroy it by targeting the municipal authorities in the bigger industrial cities.

You take some trouble to refute the notion of an underclass and no doubt *New Times* readers would agree with you in deploring use of the term as a stigmatising and evaluative concept. But maybe it has some validity as a description of the roles certain people are forced into in our society. Would you reject for example, the notion of a criminal subculture?

It is rarely a helpful one. Crime in deprived neighbourhoods is part of a broader pattern of responses to depressing and humiliating circumstances. This problem cannot be addressed unless we ensure there are opportunities for the people involved – usually young people – to make a legitimate living so they can acquire consumer goods and do the kinds of things other young people can do. When these opportunities are provided patterns of crime can change rather quickly. You are not dealing with a class, you are dealing with a situation and the situation can be changed. There are places in Glasgow where that has been achieved. Of course things can go the other way too.

Can you mention some examples of change in both directions?

The Barrowfield estate in Glasgow was 40 per cent empty a few years ago. There were serious gang fights most weekends, a murder about once a year and some horrifying rapes. The council was on the brink of demolishing the place – just giving up on it. But thanks to people who actually lived there and the support of community workers and others, that estate is now full again and the level of violence is insignificant. There are still many problems to be solved, not least unemployment, but it has got its act together in a remarkable way – and thanks very largely to the leadership of the hard men who were previously responsible for a lot of the crime. Over the same period in parts of the Hulme estate in Manchester there was a disintegration of public services and the emptying out of property, with everybody escaping who could, and an influx of new people who broke into houses and traded in drugs, a kind of jungle condition was developing. There too, many people are now working to turn things round.

And how do you turn gang leaders into responsible civic activists?

Given the right circumstances they do it for themselves. The leaders of half the states in the world have at some stage in their careers been described as terrorists.

But they usually had some political orientation from the start. The change in Barrowfield – how was it actually made?

By bringing good public service staff right into the middle of the scheme with an open door to anyone who wanted to come and talk to them; by working closely with key people in the estate and helping them to set up their own projects and developing those in quite sophisticated ways; focusing on jobs and training, more than on housing and other things which came later; by giving jobs particularly to people who had played a leading part in making trouble – but on terms which compelled them to work at the other end of the estate. It was their own idea that each side should give hostages to fortune, as it were. It could have turned out badly, but in fact it worked. And that would not have been possible without the leadership of local people who had no professional qualifications between them other than a few years in Peterhead jail and similar places.

What do you think about the effects of the inculcation into teenagers and young men of macho and selfish role models by the media, both broadcasting and tabloid press?

The media do not help, but there has been a rise in crime over the years, and much more dramatically a rise in the *fear* of crime. These are part of the broader pattern which originates first of all from poverty, inequality and the exclusion of large groups of people from the mainstream of their society. Secondly, growing poverty is particularly loaded onto families with young children, among the unemployed, low-paid workers and lone parents. So we are loading growing stresses onto youngsters at the most formative years of their lives, and onto their parents, who have to look after them. Thirdly, the most impoverished people are increasingly concentrated in neighbourhoods where public services are poor and deteriorating, and the supporting influences of a stable community get eroded and destroyed. If you add these three things together then you are bound to get problems, among which crime, though nasty, is not the most important. You also get rising illness, shorter expectation of life, poorer attainment in schools, more addiction, more family breakdown and more homelessness – a range of stresses, among which crime plays its part. It would be amazing if it did not.

Can you say something about the background to the Social Justice Commission which the Labour Party has sponsored, and your own role in relation to it?

I have no role in the sense that I am not a member, and I played no part in setting it up. I have simply talked to some of the people involved. I hope they will look at the more fundamental political issues. They have been typecast by the media as a social security and taxation commission, a 'new Beveridge', when what is needed is not simply to ask, for example, how to provide an income for the unemployed, but whether we need so many unemployed and, if not, how can we bring unemployment down? Those questions pose difficult problems for the labour movement because rising unemployment has excluded people to such an extent that they have become excluded from the political process too. They are neglected as much by powerful institutions on the left as on the right. We need greater mobility of labour and more extensive training, more and wiser investment, but also a centrally agreed wage bargaining system which restricts the growth of incomes to preserve jobs, so that we no longer use unemployment as the main regulator of the economy. When Norman Lamont said that unemployment was 'a price well worth paying' to bring inflation under control, his words were true for the relatively prosperous two-thirds of society who need to protect themselves from the effects of their own economic failure – at the expense of those who are going to lose their jobs. Unions have been more concerned to protect the wages of existing members than to look for long-term arrangements that would result in higher employment. If there are lots of people out of work, that makes it harder to achieve every progressive aim: more flexible retirement ages, better opportunities for women, equal treatment for ethnic minorities... you name it. If we have to accept the assertion that the present rates of unemployment are with us forever, progressives can go home and grow roses.

What about the argument that the market forces now embodied in international capital are so powerful that they will always crumple welfare barriers such as were built in post-war Europe, and bring into existence a pool of immiseration aimed at keeping down labour costs? Even the Swedish position has deteriorated quite seriously of late.

That may be what happens. But recent changes in Sweden are due to political decisions, not just a response to market pressures. Even conservative regimes, such as those in Germany and Japan, have been able to restrict the rise in unemployment. However, a world recession does make that much more difficult.

What is your view of the current within recent Labour Party thinking which argues the virtues of targeting benefits?

It brings back the question of levels of unemployment. We could afford a universal system of benefits – which need not necessarily mean a uniform, flat rate one – if we had levels of unemployment like we used to have. We spend such vast sums of money maintaining people in idleness, so difficult choices inevitably have to be made. It is very important to keep posing the fundamental question of whether we need to have that degree of exclusion. We may be compelled to go for more selective services just because we fail to solve the problems of unemployment – but that is a political choice not an economic necessity. We need to think in terms of collective action, rather than buying our way out whenever social problems affect us personally. If we go selective, more and more people see the public system as a drain on their own funds which they would prefer to use in buying the private option. That destroys solidarity and creates a destructive and divisive society.

If unemployment is not going to be significantly decreased, do you think there is a case for targeting benefits?

There may be, in the sense that if the ship is going down you have to take to the lifeboats. That is a response to a disaster, not a way of escaping it. If the basic, minimum level of unemployment keeps rising we are heading for social divisions and disorder on a growing scale. I hope we can confront that and turn things around while there is still time.

How about the latest Tory idea of Work Fare?

Unemployed people want to work, but not in schemes which are exploitative and threaten the jobs of people who are in properly paid employment. The effect of these schemes, if developed on a large scale, is to erode the opportunities and bargaining power of people who are still in work. That may well be the intention.

Do you feel that there is a sense of demoralisation on the left and a lack of conviction that anything can be done against the forces which want to perpetuate the existing system?

It is not clear where the impetus for justice and humane reform will re-emerge, but I am completely convinced that it will. It is important to remember that great reforming movements always ultimately fail. Times change, and new problems emerge to which the original solutions seem less relevant – and in long-established movements there are always tendencies to intellectual and spiritual corruption. We are living through a period of that sort, but it has all happened before. When Milton or Bunyan saw the Stuarts restored they did not conclude that the Puritan revolution had all been a mistake. They went on writing and when, many years later, revolution was again in the air, their writings were an inspiration once more. The failure of the Chartists in 1848 was not the end of universal suffrage and all the other things they campaigned for. Next time it may not be called 'socialism', but the passion for justice will come round again in some form or other. When the ideas of socialism were first hammered out, it was natural to see the transfer of real property – factories, land, houses – to collective ownership as the key to everything else. It was through that kind of property that capitalists wielded their power. But ownership patterns are changing, power is now wielded in new ways and we have to tackle it in new ways. Finance capital is still a real power, which now operates internationally. We are slowly and painfully learning ways of tackling these new issues. An example is the way in which Glasgow has mobilised private capital to renew the housing estates around the city on terms which keep these businesses working and employing local people, but prevent ripoffs and exploitation. We have to learn similar strategies in many other fields.

'Market socialism'?

I am not sure that 'market socialism' has a clear enough meaning. Working with the private sector in ways which are not exploitative but directed more to community values than to massive profits, is what it's about.

Anything you would like to add...?

New Times has an important part to play in providing a forum for the various potential sources of political innovation, radical thinking and protest; speaking for women, environmental groups, ethnic minorities, for a range of interests and concerns that need to mobilise and to find a way of talking to each other. It is not a question of trying to shepherd them into the labour movement, it is a matter of the labour movement having to learn from their concerns and respond to them. I have been uncertain of the future potential of trade unions as an instrument of progress. They *can* be instruments for change, but only if their members and other surrounding forces in society push them in those directions and sustain the trade unionists who want to move that way. If this paper can keep a dialogue open between the labour movement and progressive people who would never think of attending a Labour Party meeting, it will perform a great service.

POVERTY DEMOBILISES

Beatrix Campbell interviewed by **Mike Power**

Mike Power: How deep is the difference between the way we on the left viewed politics in the 1980s and how we are approaching things in the 1990s?

Beatrix Campbell: Throughout the 1980s we on the left had a strong sense of people's increasing estrangement from political parties and the political process. The notion that politics was an arena in which some real difference could be made was fracturing. By the early 1990s it completely fractured. Now people's distance from political machinery and the sense of paralysis felt within politics by left activists is acute. It is hard to imagine what is going to emerge from the political world that will impact creatively on society. That is the major difference, for the left, between now and the late 1980s, which was a period of contemplation and critique after the activism of the early 1980s, including the many wonderfully improvised forms of political struggle, and the last gasps of the great traditionalism, like the miners' strike.

We were demobilised by Thatcherism, were we not?

Yes, we were entirely wrong-footed by Thatcher and learned how even our political parties were greatly dependent on other institutions. For instance we became aware of Labour's dependence on the town hall or the central state and their resources. However, this dependence has almost run out and there is little room for manoeuvre around those state institutions. Now, apart from the SWP and Class War there is very little 'left' activism, of the mobilising on the streets, paper selling, kick-it, smash-it, stuff-it variety. The attention directed towards what was modernising in British society missed a substantial part of the population that was poor and apparently not living a life that was on the leading edge of metropolitan change. In the 1980s there was the re-emergence of a new notion of 'undeserving' poor and an increase in the respectable, legitimate poor, but it was not attracting much political attention on the left, which had historically been attracted to the victim as an icon. We recognised that we could not simply animate left energy by constant reference to people who are worse off, or more degraded than ourselves.

The idea of oppression and referring to people as victims is still very much in the language of the left. But surely we need to identify where people are effectively responding and successfully resolving their problems. How people in their communities are recognising that the political process and its parties have failed them and are acting together in a spirit of self-help. They are not just laying down and saying, 'I am victim', but are fighting back.

People will always do what people have always done – they will put a life together. They will do this in dialogue with the people they live with; their neighbourhood; the resources and institutions to which they have access; the religions they adhere to; and the state discourse that comes across on the telly every day. So the positive thing about the departure of the victim as an icon, in terms of mainstream left thought, was that it never corresponded to what working class life was like anyway. People were constructing ways of life that the 'respectable', the 'organised' were not necessarily in touch with. Yet even we were doing it in our own way – getting on with life that is, though not in forms of survival that could be inscribed in a 'movement' terminology.

Yes, we wanted the big global, universalistic solutions to everything. We said, 'Don't worry, these things may be a problem now but they will all be solved when we achieve socialism.' This was still in the political psyche of most of us.

Completely. And we did not know how to deal with complicated situations that arose from this. For instance, many people lived on badly managed council estates that were starved of resources, but they could not even have a rent strike, because most had their rent paid through housing benefit. So their opportunity for resistance was nil, unlike in the 1950s or earlier. This meant that our 'big idea' did not correspond with people's experience. Now we have tenants' associations being opportunistically created by the Labour

Party to get support for local authority tenure of the estates. This has nothing to do with what tenants might actually feel like doing in their associations, but is an exercise in Labour attempting to protect its political base.

Therefore is this political alienation of ordinary people that you identified, which took place in the second half of the 1980s, going to get worse as the 1990s progress?

Yes. And at the same time we are watching a rate of disintegration in Eastern Europe that we would not have predicted in 1989. This means we are seeing Europe being reshaped in ways that make many people ask: 'What kind of Europe am I going to be living in? Will there be another war?' Those of us who grew up in the 1960s and thought we were the peace generation are now wondering if we will have to experience what our parents went through. This is a bewildering moment. Meanwhile at home there is the growing prospect of four million officially unemployed. We already have two generations of young people who live in a culture of entrenched unemployment. There are neighbourhoods in every city in Britain where most young people have never had a job. But these young people are completely plugged in to a national culture – more so than your average political activist. They watch the telly, know what is going on, and know what is available – but cannot have any of it. So, on many council estates there is an unofficial, illegal system of circulating goods that gives people access to the minimum conditions of a social life – a video, a telly, a washing machine. Anything can be got. It is an illicit economy which most people in most poor, peripheral estates are implicated in; they live an 'off-the-back-of-the-lorry' existence. The estates are serviced by low-level loan sharks who take a phenomenal portion of those neighbourhoods' weekly income. There are no banks nearby, nor the standard services of the average high street.

It would be quite wrong, given the number of people in this situation, to ask: what stake have they got in our society? The real question is: what does that situation produce for those people? And what kind of power therefore prevails over their neighbourhoods?

Exactly. And after 13 years in which this has been relentlessly consolidated it is clear that they have been abandoned by a political system that regards them as 'a great open mouth', that is either hungry or shouting and generally clamouring. So their needs are being constantly policed by the people who should be servicing them, but the servicers often do not see the strengths that exist in these neighbourhoods. These are systems of informal solidarities which are about creative support, and which are generally run by mothers. They include things like mothers' and toddlers' groups, small scale co-ops, groups recycling secondhand goods, community enterprises, and a growing number of credit unions and other cooperative initiatives. This is a modest renaissance of the co-op tradition which had stopped thinking about a democratic form of consumption. On many of these estates can be seen tiny, under-resourced, struggling co-ops being run by women. By contrast there are autonomous structures of a crime economy. This is illegal, informal and hard, even brutal when it feels the need to be. The other is solidaristic, communitarian, practical, useful and insofar as it is able to be, democratic. Often the two are in tension, with the latter besieged by the 'lads' who sustain the criminal economy, as well as by state institutions, because it is critical and sometimes radical. The 'lads' are interesting – plugged in to mainstream values, often quite Thatcherite, in that they care about 'having' and do not care about consequences. Their systems are run by heavy-duty men, who will do anything to maintain their personal and economic power; they are macho and exclusive. The two cooperative and criminal systems are not compatible. The political failure to wrap some support and sense of authority around that communitarian solidarity and survival means that the strongholds of those communities are identified as being with the dangerous boys. They are not 'dangerous estates', but are places living with contradictory modes of survival.

Are the people you refer to those in the bottom 'one-third' of our 'one-third two-thirds society' who are excluded from politics by the way in which it has been professionalised and adopted an exclusive language?

Actually the bottom third is now more like 40 per cent and growing, not least in the Tory voting southeast. Meanwhile the exclusion from politics was revealed by how small the constituency was that came out in support of the services that Labour felt it wanted to defend, such as health, education or general welfare. This is partly because people felt so ill served by those services, and because the Labour Party and movement rely on a mood of defence, which is about defending their jobs and thereby the services. But what we need are services that are dynamic, creative and at the advanced edge of society. Unfortunately these features are usually only applied to making profit, while service always seems to be represented as conservative by nature. Therefore the driving force in service provision has to be the relationship with the consumer. And what has not been resolved since World War II and has been in crisis for the past dozen years is what kind of dialogue will there be between the users and providers of services. We are now faced with debates about public service that are either rhetorical and abstract, or they are professionalised and part of a professional language. For instance what was the 'great education debate' about? Does the average person or school student have the faintest idea? They are not clear about what is being tested, or what is being yielded, or what they could do either politically or personally with the information. What are massively significant political arguments have become contained in a professionalised discourse, which excludes the community at large. The same is true of the 'debate' about the Maastricht treaty, few people have a clue what that is about. This situation paralyses the average political activist who usually acts on the assumption that they know what they think.

That describes how the political relationship has broken down, particularly on the estates. But what about the left? It does not seem to be able to do anything about this.

Well the activist left does not live there. It is also exhausted in terms of ideas as well as energy. Anyway political power is somewhere else, it is not with the 40 per cent. Its problems are intractable. For example a demand is made of a local authority – and when it is turned down, then what? Nobody knows what to do. There has been a strategic series of cuts and the estates have seen their services slowly erode. This means that people's needs are increasing, which makes their problems, and those of political activists about how to address them, even more acute.

Finally then, do we need to start thinking about the poor in the way we used to in the 1930s, 1940s and 1950s? You say we are not among the poor, so how do we approach the problem?

We have to start by acknowledging that Britain is a place that has stopped being able to recognise itself – it does not know who it is. It is remarkable how the sense of class belonging has remained unchanged throughout the period you mention. Today 60 per cent in Britain still think they are working class. The trouble is we no longer know what that means. It is no longer connected to political institutions that express working class consciousness or culture. And there remain big divergences within working class culture, as well as working class respectability. The cultural divergences have become amplified by gender, generational, regional and racial differences and unless left politics gets to grips with, and learns to manage, that extraordinary development of diversity that operates within the working class, they will continue to miss the point of modern politics. The informal institutions in poor neighbourhoods, which really express their strengths, have to be supported. This challenges the ambiguous relationship that the political institutions have with them. And it is in the gift of the institutions to make decisions that could be crucial in resourcing generous and democratic activities. The poor are hovering between aspirations and disaster.

STRONG MEDICINE

Dr Steve Iliffe interviewed by **Dom Ford**

Dom Ford: Two years into the government's health service reforms we are in the midst of what the BMA calls the worst crisis in 30 years. The Tory reforms have only aggravated the underlying crises in the NHS, but after the election, trusts, GP fundholders and the market are here to stay. How do you see the Tories' agenda developing?

Dr Steve Iliffe: The political row about funding healthcare will plague the government for the foreseeable future, becoming so intense that they will have to find a way of raising large sums of money to pump into the system. It is possible that they could go down the privatisation road, but who in the City is going to fund it, given the state of the economy and the experience of privatised health services elsewhere, particularly in the US? It is unlikely that the private sector could be brought in as a partner and provide large slabs of resources, except perhaps in London and the south east. So the only other route is public funding. Advocates of the reforms are worried that Virginia Bottomley is backtracking. They are right to be worried because what Bottomley is now doing is attempting to manage the market, and she may be as successful at doing this as Gorbachev was in converting Soviet socialism to modern socialism. Arguably she should let the market rip. But the political fall out from this may be too much for the Conservatives to handle, which is why the Tomlinson Report appeared. The Community Care Act is the same. The market has been sucking public money into private residential homes in ever greater amounts, so it has to be regulated. This is what the Community Care Act is about; the regulation of that flow of money and the reduction of services to large sections of the population at the same time.

David Blunkett says he would get rid of trusts and GP fundholders but at the same time keep an open mind on the internal market. Is this a realistic response to the reforms?

It may not be easy to get rid of trusts just like that and GP fundholders might do it for themselves either by amalgamating into very large units or by going bust. This checklist of counter-reforms, while vaguely realistic in the run up to the last election, is unrealistic now. What is needed is to increase the proportion of the Gross National Product spent on health to the European level of around 8 per cent. The health service now has a European-style health service bureaucracy without European-style money. With regard to the purchaser/provider split, in a situation of greater resources it might work. Perhaps we should think about taking the right literally and saying let the money follow the patient by giving the money to the patients and seeing how they spend it.

And beyond that?

The left needs to think more closely about democracy and health care. To me this means having a way of communicating with people in a locality to find out their different interests and needs, and in that way initiating a debate about their perspectives, needs and wants − not in the sense of here is your list of options tick them 1 to 472, rather an input of ideas from all sectors of the population. Public discussions about rationing are problematic. First, the wishes of the articulate middle classes may dominate. Second, public discussion can also reflect popular prejudice about whether services should be provided for, say, people living with HIV and AIDS. Democracy does not mean that the 'public' rules. To me that is essentially a right-wing attitude − you mobilise a group of people and they express their prejudices. Democracy can mean arguing and understanding an issue and reaching decisions on the basis of consensus. This means accepting that some people will not like it and will not benefit as much as they should do. Implicit in this idea of democracy are notions of solidarity, altruism and self-discipline. One problem is that this society is splitting into two groups − put crudely, the young and well and the old and ill, who have very different perspectives and needs. The left could try to bridge the gap between the two groups. Today many people want homeopathy on the NHS, but not necessarily at the expense of chiropody. A brake must be put on the social pressures that drive one group of people towards a solution to these problems at the expense of their neighbours.

Rationing of health care has so far been covert and implicit but the under-resourcing of the Community Care reforms will bring priority-setting sharply into focus, because people whose needs are deemed to be low or moderate, even though they are very real, will find it more and more difficult to access services. This is a huge problem because it is a deliberate government policy to make the social services into a safety net for those in extreme need. The same sort of thing may not apply in quite that way to the health service because it has a broader remit and touches a larger population. But if we have an inalienable right to health care we have to think about what health care is. Is it something the pharmaceutical industry or the surgical supply industry can define or is it something we can debate and describe in political terms? I favour the latter but suspect that what will happen is the continuation of the old order where what is health is determined by the medico-pharmaceutical complex, which will always draw more money to itself, to its own advantage.

The government has to a limited extent taken on board the progressive ideas of the Health for All Movement with its Health of the Nation initiative, where for the first time health is related to every aspect of government – transport, housing, the environment and employment. How do you see this?

The strength of Conservatism lies in its capacity to absorb the ideas of its opponents and of the preceding era, turn them round and adapt them to its perspective of a society based on cash relationships. The Health of the Nation is an example of how a kind of planning perspective can be turned to the advantage of the right. What is not coming through very strongly, and probably will take a very long time to emerge, is a civil society which sees itself as pursuing health goals rather than having health delivered by an institution. Obviously, some things need to be delivered. For example, there is no DIY hip replacement. But for the younger and healthier population, the issues really need to be dealt with not by professional services, which is the right-wing perspective, but by civil society. Whether or not you get bronchitis through passive smoking is not a problem for the local GP but an issue for you within your community and social relationships. We are only on the edge of coming out of the statist perception of health. We all think of these sort of things being provided for us to make us better and the government does that brilliantly. For example, it packages health promotion as a thing which is done to you. GPs are supposed to promote people's health, just as sheep farmers dip sheep. This is an absurd idea, but it fits in neatly with having a private gynaecologist or other private specialists who guide you through the intricacies of decision making for a small fee. Everything is itemised and then turned into a commodity.

If the right has repackaged some of the ideas of the left how can we take the agenda back? In your book *Strong Medicine* (London: Laurence and Wishart, 1988) you proposed some heretical ideas which were not taken up at the time.

No, people on the left thought they were right wing ideas. Now they are here because the Conservatives are powerful and successful in a way many of us never thought they could be. It turns out that they were probably more in touch with the nature of society than we were. But I doubt that they can deliver. Bottomley and Tomlinson are bottling out of Thatcher's plan and trying to go back to some kind of planned mixed economy of health care. We should not let them get away with 'regressive modernisation'; we should advocate progress. For example, in the twenty-first century people ought to be able to carry their medical record on a smart card or know what proportion of their income is being spent on the health service and what that provides. In this way people would have more control over their health. These things are feasible within the existing technology but the left is very conservative on this.

On democracy the left agenda goes no further than who should sit on district health authorities.

Absolutely, but this is irrelevant. Elected health authorities could have the most appalling people on them. I do not want my local council replicated on the health authority – I live in the London Borough of Brent. Democracy is about participation, in my view. The essence of democracy is what you contribute, what you learn and what you teach, which works best at a local level. And there the issue is knowing what local services there are and making some kind of contribution to them or having an existing contribution made explicit. We pay miserable sums of money to people to look after those who are infirm. That should be a waged job. Arguably anybody who is looking after small children should be given a wage just for doing it. Child benefit is a poor attempt at that. You can make an argument for a citizen's wage. For example, I am going to look after this person here who happens to be 2, or 42 but has multiple sclerosis, or 82 but with dementia. And that is my social task. And I am drawn into that by local government which pays me to do it. That would seem to me to be part of an operative democracy, a participatory democracy.

You have described yourself as a card carrying defeatist. Is this still the case or are you more optimistic for the future of the National Health Service?

We have been defeated! There is a temptation on the left simply to redouble one's faith when confronted with evidence that you are wrong. This is a religious way of thinking. Yet paradoxically the potential for change is now greater than it was 10 years ago. We have not been defeated in our capacity to argue the issues and many of the deeply conservative structures of the post-war period – including the NHS – are open to change. There are things about clarification of information and dissemination of ideas where we have a very strong hand. Transferring power and responsibility to the periphery of the health service, which is what the government has done, admittedly without sufficient resources, has actually allowed some progressive people to do more than they have ever been able to do before in terms of provision of local services. These things are individually very small but when added together are potentially big. When we remember that the current administration is unlikely to deliver its promises about the NHS, we might spot opportunities for the left. The initiative could return to us sooner that we think, provided that we abandon our sentimental attachments to the old order.

PART FOUR

BEYOND THE PARTY POLITICAL:
A RADICAL AGENDA FOR DEMOCRACY

For a Radical Democracy

Adam Lent

THE IDEOLOGICAL MENU continues to shrink. Thatcherism is the latest doctrine to face discredit and rejection. But Maggie's creed is only one in a long list of political positions that have increasingly lost their power to explain and guide in the last 30 years. Radical socialism is regarded simultaneously as quaint and doctrinaire, social democracy as visionless and dull, paternalist Toryism is espoused by a dying generation, and John Major's confused brand of pragmatism never gained enough support in the first place to suffer discredit. These are, of course, generalisations but there can be no doubt that the traditional ideological options of this century seem increasingly unable to provide credible solutions to the problems and needs of Europe and Britain as they enter the next century.

There are a wide variety of reasons for this situation. Changes in the global economy have left national governments with less economic power; the decline of traditional class structures and identities has removed the social bases from which political parties gained their most active support; and the end of the cold war has destroyed the major legitimation for western unity and ideological hawkishness. But the last 30 years has also seen the gradual growth of two major issues to which none of the great political doctrines have been able to react satisfactorily. These are the issues of difference and inequality.

The issue of difference refers to the dual problem for state and society of responding to the demands of a wide variety of differing identities and values while simultaneously maintaining and developing the integration that contemporary economies and cultures require. The issue of difference was originally most visible with the growth of ethnic communities and the failure of public authorities to respond in any way other than through disenfranchisement and racism. However, since the 1960s there has been a growing willingness on the part of individuals and groups to acknowledge openly their own uniqueness and to fight against the structures and beliefs that either prevent the development of their uniqueness or discriminate on the grounds of their difference. Radical movements built around sexuality, gender, disability, race, religion, culture, age, locality and lifestyle continue to provide the most challenging and exciting politics of recent decades. However, neither the conservative nor the progressive ideologies and institutions of the mainstream have shown themselves willing or able to take up the challenge of difference. This is largely because the consciousness of difference has itself developed with the recognition that the apparently liberatory politics of parliamentary socialism have a tendency towards an authoritarianism and patriarchy that can be just as stifling for difference as the values of conservatism.

This disillusion with mainstream progressive politics is linked to the issue of inequality. Despite 50 years of a campaigning and powerful parliamentary socialism, British society is still riven by great inequalities in *all* spheres of life. However, social democracy and parliamentary socialism have concentrated their attempts to limit inequality almost exclusively on the sphere of economic relations. This has not only meant that inequalities in political, cultural and social relations have been reproduced by supposedly progressive forces but that opportunities have remained for reactionary powers, like Thatcherism, to use unequal power resources – such as centralised political authority – to deconstruct the gains that were made by the labour movement. The belief that ending economic inequality was more vital than ending inequality elsewhere and that progressive economic changes would automatically promote progressive changes in other spheres has been disproved. A far more realistic approach is the goal of 'total equality', where attempts to limit inequality take place in political, cultural, and social relations as well as the economic. However, this approach of total equality requires a reassessment of the way equality is conceived – the social democratic goal of redistributive economic equality[1] cannot be generalised to all other spheres of life. More about this below.

The importance of these two fundamental issues have revealed themselves most clearly in the 'new politics', the diverse movements and ideals that have developed in response to the failings of mainstream politics. This new politics exists in the social movements mentioned above, the growth of ecological campaigns and Green ideals, a burgeoning concern with autonomy and diversity as in traveller communities and 'freedom to party' campaigns, and the increasing frequency of community self-help associations such as LET schemes, credit unions and cooperatives. All of these movements and trends are responses to the challenges of difference and inequality. Movements shaped by gender, ethnicity, sexuality, disability, age etc. are not only attempts to prevent discrimination on the grounds of difference but have played the leading role in dignifying the uniqueness of various communities and asserting that uniqueness as a good in itself. Alongside Green ideas and campaigns these movements have increasingly valued the right to control one's destiny and environment while fighting exclusion from, and subordination in, spheres of life such as cultural practice, social interaction and political activity. Furthermore, the recent growth of the self-help associations mentioned above is also providing the earliest indications of a new politics response to the traditionally socialist preserve of economic problems. The implications and demands of this new politics are not met by any of the mainstream, or even any of the fringe, ideologies on offer. As a result the new politics remains fragmented as a movement. Such fragmentation is not all bad, it ensures that the authoritarianism of the historical labour movement has not been repeated. However, it also means that the new politics has failed to present any profound and prolonged challenge to dominant ideologies and structures.

Nevertheless, the ideals and practice of the new politics and the issues of difference and inequality themselves do suggest a possible set of common political goals that can be labelled 'radical democracy'. These common political goals include the extension of democratic processes beyond the political sphere, the defence and encouragement of pluralism in all aspects of contemporary life, the development of 'differential citizenship',[2] and the aim of a complex and total equality.[3] These goals are dealt with in turn below.

The existence of different identities, beliefs, and lifestyles ensures that conflict, the desire for autonomy and problems of integration play a major role in present-day society. Democratic processes – as in the structures linked to accountability, equal votes and elections – have been fundamental for Europe in responding to these facts of difference. However, these democratic processes remain limited to a very narrow, political sphere while centres of authoritarianism exist *throughout* society. As a result a democratic response to conflict, autonomy and integration is not a feature of most of the largest associations of contemporary life. The great agencies of the state – such as welfare structures, the police, the judiciary, the education system, the civil service, the military – remain monolithic, bureaucratic and absolutist. The introduction of democratic processes into these agencies would obviously ensure greater reflection of difference and less authoritarian modes of integration. A similar point can be made about business and industry which remain almost totally untouched by any form of democratic process.

But democratic processes must be buttressed by a rich political culture based on understanding, diversity and active public debate. The burden for this must rest with the mass media and the education system. The media should be subject to far greater diversity in control and in views expressed, while the education system must link its training in organisational and intellectual skills to the needs and demands of the wide variety of communities it serves.[4] The failure to develop such a rich political culture ensures that democratic processes become corrupt, clientist and unused by those they should be serving.

However, there are also spheres of life where authoritarianism still pervades but where the introduction of traditional democratic processes would be inappropriate. These include cultural practices based on personal taste and creative freedom, and social relations such as the family or sexual partnerships. In these areas pluralism must be encouraged and defended to ensure that democracy is entrenched. This might involve providing the time, training and resources for contributions by those who are rarely represented in cultural practice. It also requires the enforcement of the right of individuals and groups to enter into any consenting social relationship of their choosing. This may mean going beyond the simple liberal prescription of avoiding legislation on areas that are to be based on free choice towards discovering ways of deconstructing the in-built bias in our society towards certain types of social relationship.

Diversity in economic relations must also be encouraged, ensuring that differing modes of distribution and production are possible. As has been pointed out above this is already happening in a small way with the growth of LET schemes, credit unions and cooperatives. Removing the bias that maintains certain modes of existence will be a slow process but it must be a process that is conducted by the marginalised themselves. The belief that is prevalent in social democracy that politicians or technocrats can simply extend new rights to those who are 'badly-off' must be rejected. However, while disenfranchised groups can to an extent take the initiative on building their own communities and identities free from interference, there is a strong sense in which a democratic society is inevitably one that is highly integrated – based on complex interactions, compromise and conflict. Ensuring that historically disenfranchised groups can take part in that integrated process on equal terms is the issue most central to 'differential citizenship'.

This notion of citizenship, developed most recently by Iris Marion Young,[5] argues that traditional liberal notions of a universal citizenship based upon what everyone supposedly has in common – that is, their active involvement in the public sphere – in fact benefits the particular needs of the dominant group of white, middle-class, able-bodied, heterosexual males. Young argues that to rectify this situation three elements must be built in to democratic processes: the provision of resources for the self-organisation of disenfranchised groups; the requirement that decision makers consult such groups and prove they have taken their perspective into account; and the right of groups to veto legislation that has a direct bearing on their well-being. To this one might add the right of certain groups to establish a legally semi-autonomous relationship to the state and society. Some communities of travellers might be prime candidates for such a relationship.

Clearly, the three aspects of a radical conception of democracy outlined above are ways of responding to demands for greater reflection of difference and for greater equality in all spheres of life – total equality. But obviously the extension of democratic processes and pluralism and developments in notions of citizenship does not amount to a vision of equality that is identical to that of the traditional progressive notion of equality. This traditional progressive notion, developed by socialist theorists and politicians, is based primarily on the redistribution of economic resources. However, it is a notion that must be revised if democracy is to be the key principle in developing the new politics and in renewing a radical project. Redistribution of the dominant social good – economic resources – has historically required an extension of state power beyond that which is acceptable if the principles outlined above are to hold full sway. A new question about equality should be asked by any progressive project: not 'How can economic equality be achieved in the quickest and most far reaching way?' but rather 'How can equality be established in *all* spheres of life in the most democratic way?' The former question often seems the most forthright and purposeful but, as has been indicated above, it is usually self-contradictory since achieving economic equality through, for example, the strong state only leads to new inequalities in other spheres or simply leaves the whole project open to abuse and assault by non-egalitarian forces.

In his book, *Spheres of Justice*,[6] Michael Walzer proposes a form of equality he calls 'complex equality'. This approach rejects the idea of redistributing one dominant social good to achieve equality and instead suggests that equality resides in ensuring that different criteria are used to distribute different goods in different spheres. Instead of money simply being redistributed from rich to poor, major commodities might be distributed according to wealth, while health is distributed according to need, education is distributed to all freely, and political power according to electoral success. Walzer suggests that if such divisions between spheres of distribution are strictly maintained then while inequalities might arise within each sphere, those inequalities would not be reproduced across all spheres. For example, the wealthy individual might be able to buy the best television set but s/he would not also necessarily have the best health care or the greatest political power; those goods might be the province of a less materially wealthy individual. While this vision does indicate a useful development for new conceptions of equality, it is never made clear by Walzer how this 'complex equality' is to be achieved. However, if we ask ourselves the question outlined above – 'How can equality be established in all spheres of life in the most democratic way?' – we see that the equality that might arise is a complex form of Walzer's 'complex equality'.

If social change is brought about through grassroots initiative, through voluntary association (as it must be to remain democratic), we might find that different ways of distributing social goods would exist not only from sphere to sphere but actually within spheres as well. Major commodities would be distributed according to wealth by some, according to need by others and used communally by another community. A mixture of private health care and free health care may exist in one community while another may dispense with private medicine altogether and yet another may devise a wholly new way of distributing health care based possibly on a large-scale shift to prevention rather than cure.

Of course it is vital to remember that such a vision of equality can only begin to be credible in a situation of radical democracy where no particular group can maintain the status quo through an entrenched hold on power – whatever mode of distribution that is chosen it must be challengeable at one or more levels of social organisation. Furthermore, it is simply one vision of equality. It cannot amount to a blueprint and if the socialist conception of equality is anything to go by it will require constant refinement in practice to ensure that it remains workable and true to its goals.

This piece has attempted, very briefly, to outline some basic principles for a radical conception of democracy. It is only one possible political response to the issues of difference and inequality. But it is a response that might provide a clearer political direction to some of the diverse and fragmented movements and individuals that make up the 'New Politics'. The late twentieth century is unique in that the growth of political disillusion and discredit has not resulted in a consequent support for any coherent radical alternatives. As was indicated above, this is partly because the traditional radical, progressive vision of the world seems as irrelevant as that of the mainstream. What might be the outcome of a period of such disillusion it is difficult to say; early indications seem to be that only the entrenched traditions of xenophobia, racism and nationalism may continue to benefit. Such circumstances make it all the more vital that those involved in the defending and dignifying of communities attempt, at least, limited forms of cohesion so as to present a juster and more hopeful vision of the future than those presently on offer.

Notes:

1. For an outline and critique of 'simple equality', see: M. Walzer, *Spheres of Justice: A Defence of Pluralism and Equality*, Oxford: Basil Blackwell, 1983, pp.3-20.

2. For an outline of 'differential citizenship' see: I. M. Young, *Polity and Group Difference: A Critique of the Ideal of Universal Citizenship*, Ethics, no. 99 (January 1989) pp. 250-74.

3. For an outline of 'complex equality', see: M. Walzer, 'Spheres of Justice'.

4. For a very useful account of how education can democratically link its role to the needs of a community see: G. & C. Kirkwood, *Living Adult Education*, Milton Keynes: Open University Press in association with the Scottish Institute of Adult and Continuing Education, 1989.

5. I. M. Young, *Polity and Group Difference*.

EMBRACING EQUALITY AND DIFFERENCE

Anne Showstack Sassoon interviewed by **Anne Coddington**

Anne Coddington: Your ideas seem to 'celebrate' difference, which is a far cry from the universalist and collectivist thinking that socialists and communists have promoted in the past, usually at the expense of acknowledging individual needs. How will comprehending 'difference' and equality enhance the struggle for social change and transformation?

Anne Showstack Sassoon: We must start from an understanding that society is multifarious and differentiated, whereas notions such as equality before the law, as important as they are, are abstract and universal, which obscures the fact that difference plays an important part when individuals compete under the same set of rules. When we impose these universal categories on differences, some people will inevitably become marginalised. We have, therefore, to struggle for equality, but we also have to reconcile this struggle with problems like how, say, a working woman or man with young children finds space and flexible reactions in the workplace to take account of their specificity. So the old ideas need to be placed in a new context, and we need to enrich and develop new approaches towards them. It is interesting here to think about the daily lives of people: for example how they relate to the state in all its forms, from their connections with law and order to the welfare state and its institutions such as schools. And thinking about my own life and that of other women in this way it strikes me that we need to continue to struggle to make equality before the law, which is a very old liberal idea, a reality, for example, for black people and women, while clearly understanding that each of us has different social needs. We relate to the welfare state's institutions differently depending on where we are in the life cycle; whether we have children; or whether an individual's background makes their approach to the welfare state problematic. This is the real, differentiated context of our citizenship, of our relationship to the state whatever our social and political rights. Therefore the monolithic, statist social democratic, or East European communist/socialist approaches are not only redundant but also unhelpful in preparing a new left project. What we need is one which incorporates flexibility and sensitivity.

Does inserting difference mean challenging the old notions of citizenship?

Yes. We have to seek a citizenship more like that which exists in the Nordic countries, where it has been expanded to include social rights. These include rights to certain educational standards, of not suffering poverty, to good quality welfare services and has resulted in greater democratic participation in schools and local communities. This expansion has taken place in Europe, but because this country has a long liberal tradition and as a result still tends to relate more to the American experience, it has not incorporated the social dimension. We should realise that the way debates are formulated has a historical and cultural dimension. The debate in this country is influenced by the US partly because we have a common language. What strikes me as someone who grew up in the US, however, is that Britain is very European, not just because it belongs to the EC, but because of many labour movement and social democratic traditions. By that I am not thinking in terms of party politics, but in people's assumptions and expectations about the welfare state, which are very different from the attitudes in the US. We must develop a 'social citizenship' which reflects the reality of people's lives. Unfortunately, too much of the debate about citizenship is so abstract that it is millions of miles away from that reality.

Where is the demand for such a re-evaluation coming from?

It is arising from the social forces and movements in society that are demanding change. Consider, for example, the position of women. They will never achieve equality if they are simply treated like men. After all, millions of women combine working with childcare responsibilities, which means that we cannot view equality in absolute terms and we have to give priority to concepts like difference in relation to institutions and the law. Citizenship must therefore take account of gender among many other things, and developing those new concepts should be part of the left's project.

In that case can we summarise why we specifically need a new concept of citizenship?

Being a citizen in Britain today is, above all, about a legal definition. It is based on the liberal notion that everyone who is a citizen is, in principle, equal before the law regardless of race, gender or socio-economic position; that we have constitutional rights, and are part of the community. So it is a universalist notion: yet the terrain in which this is exercised emerges from the relationship we have to the rules of the welfare state. These include educational institutions and health services, which are 'the state on the ground'. And that is where 'difference' arises. The universalist notion produces a range of contradictions, but still remains an essential part of our political vocabulary, our conceptual framework, and the reality in which we live. Nevertheless it is inadequate and we have to take account of how people relate to the welfare state differentially and according to their needs, not to speak of the cultural and ethnic specifics of each of us. These are the terms in which we have to reconceptualise and incorporate difference.

How then do we go about creating a political terrain in which we can assert the positive potential of difference?

Not by trying to come up with ultimate, homogeneous compromises of the general good where differences are thrown into the melting pot and disappear. Of course we need to compromise, to share and to co-exist but we are never going to get rid of differences, and must realise that we can learn from people on the 'margins' who are different from us. To give you an example, a Finnish feminist told me that at a New York conference the dominant idea was that women from Eastern Europe were there to learn from western feminists, and women from Latin America or Africa or India should talk to each other, rather than all women learning from different experiences. The universal notion of feminism came from Anglo Saxon women who had nothing to learn from other countries. We must study the specificities of our own societies so that we can relate different realities to our own situation. We have to learn to have a transnational sense of possibilities and potential about the way people think and feel. At the same time, in constructing a political campaign relating to social forces we have to be realistic about where people are at, because the delineations of what is possible has its roots in a history and an experience that involves institutions as they are now where national traditions are terribly important.

If we open up perspectives, which is a good thing, how would we know which one might serve as a useful political strategy?

Where do we want to get to? We can't get an answer by some abstract process. We need to see the contradictions of the society as a whole. For example, millions of women are in paid work – it's a material need. Societies are structured around it. If women stopped work tomorrow society wouldn't function, but what are the conditions in which they do it? In Britain, they do it without good back up of nursery care, yet paid work is built on a model which assumes we can forget about all these other responsibilities. We should also ask what's going on in the lives of millions of people. One of the ways we try to arrive at that is through this academic world, which is all too often isolated and detached, and another way is through political parties. Those social democratic or communist parties that were rooted in society had some sense of what was going on for people in local communities, which does not happen anymore, be it the communist party as it was in Italy or the Labour Party in Britain. We do not have those threads out like we used to, and we cannot reconstruct them in the old model, but we need to have those ears on the ground. So when we think of the new strategy and we think about movements and pluralism it is very positive because we are trying to construct a relationship between groups that is not sectarian. But we have to be sensitive to the fact that these groups may or may not have roots in the wider society. They may say they represent certain interests but we have to ask to what extent they do. All the queries that came out of the GLC are not just right-wing attacks on unrepresentative groups and minorities. It is not just a questioning of representation in a formal sense, but of what information they bring to the political process.

Is there a need then to build a new socialist politics that takes difference into account? And, if so, how do we go about it?

We have got to study, think about and query the very questions we are asking. And we have to look at existing political institutions and see the spaces within them where people who may not consider themselves to be politically active are trying to create something new and better. For example, we can see a contradiction at work in the way the new universities are facing severe economic constraints and yet have adopted policies to expand. So we have had to think about how to work to engage students in an educational process which is no longer the one we are used to and guarantee quality and integrity in what we offer. What we are trying to do is think of new teaching methods and ways of working which enable students to take a more active role. Students are resources bringing something into the institution and they can help each other in new ways. There is a subversive and progressive potential within these pressures, which says that we as lecturers are not the only experts, and there are all sorts of resources out there. We become facilitators. We help structure the process which becomes more democratic, more of an exchange. We can even teach better, and students who take more responsibility can gain in self-confidence and learn better.

So what we are talking about is empowering people to realise new possibilities?

Exactly, but we have been empowered ourselves because we have been encouraged to think and rethink how we work. The present conditions of financial constraint and politically difficult conditions of always having to defend what you do means that you are forced to think creatively. The recent polemic around the GCSE is in part an example of a challenge to what we might consider an achievement of the educational system. Teachers have kept young people engaged in an examination process that has been constantly undermined. I do not want to put too optimistic a gloss on this but there is some very good work going on near the ground, and we have to be in touch with this. It is part of a vision of a more democratic society. We are talking about what is going on in workplaces, and about people's needs, and we have to recognise where the new spaces for empowerment are. This is no longer a question of advocacy or promoting a political line, but it is something we have to try to get in touch with which is going on in the context of, but not because of, political intervention. Ironically, we have to find out what people are creating within a process of change propelled, but not controlled, by the Conservatives.

Well and good, but how can we begin to do this?

If I can use an old-fashioned term, we have to have a dialectical view. We must be constantly on the look out for developments that are negative and are undermining some of the social values that we want to preserve, but we must also be aware that these developments can create new possibilities. Too often we only look for the negative elements, but we need to realise that there are also new possibilities. For example, what kind of empowering is going on, and how can we maximise the positive aspects of these developments? We have to honestly ask: how can we realise that we are only part of this process? And recognise that society is fairly impervious to policy and policy makers and politicians. To a large extent it escapes the effects of politician's intentions. This is true of the right and it would be true of the left as well. Society is so complex and has such momentum, that it is hard to get it to go in another direction. At the end of the day policy has to be translated on the ground by millions of people, and these people and institutions have deep-rooted ideas as well as the capacity to respond creatively to whatever they face. Our task is to have some kind of influence that these processes go in positive directions.

Now can we turn to what we have witnessed with the crumbling of 'communism' in the former USSR and its demise in Eastern Europe. Is the transformation that Marx envisaged to a society beyond capitalism possible?

Not in the sense of a forecast or prediction of communism ensuing from a specific class. But inserted in many of the contradictions we are living through at the moment there is a material and concrete need for a different kind of society. For example, to mention ecological problems is not just being trendy. How can we imagine a different ecosystem without a revolutionary transformation in the way the economy is managed and without changing the role of the state and the international system or our values and ways of living. Or we could look at the way work is organised and ignores responsibilities outside the world of production. There is a fundamental contradiction here and a need for a completely different model of work.

In the past we could describe an alternative to this as some kind of communism. But the language is not something we can adopt because it is associated with old regimes even if I'd argue that Marx can still teach us a thing or two. There is also a crying need to manage our planet's ecology, and of trying to build democratic terrains on which to struggle so that we can take on difference in a positive and creative way. And this demands a different kind of society. This should not just be in our imaginations, or some kind of utopia. What does seem to be utopian is that the political conditions don't seem to exist at the moment to realise it. And neither the working class as such or any political party is likely to be the agent of transformation because changes are taking place beyond class in an interaction between the economic and social spheres. There are many different agents. But if I see something in the future it is an absolute need for a different way of living. And our political task should be to build links from where we are now, and that encapsulates those needs, to a transformed society. In that way we would empower ourselves to resolve some contradictions, but that does not mean that others would not continue to arise. The real challenge is how we can create a system and a process so that these contradictions can be dealt with in a democratic way.

What do you think that Democratic Left can do to begin to develop a new democratic vision of society that is based around these notions of equality, difference and empowerment?

Democratic Left has been positive in trying to go beyond the limitations of the political tradition of the Communist Party, even though there were some very good traditions there as well. The communist tradition recognised that any political strategy must be rooted in the dynamics of society. This was never a tradition of the Labour Party, influenced as it has been by Fabian ideas of getting the policies right, talking to the experts and creating a more rational way of organising things from on high. So you must start by facing the contradictions you are living with and try to get beyond them by investigating the possibilities and dynamics of society in its multiplicity. Another area is to continue the positive contribution *Marxism Today* made in attempting to understand the logic and insights of a whole range of people (including those it considered political enemies) be it in *New Times* or by organising seminars. You should attempt to broaden the horizons of the left, in a profound and imaginative way, which I do not see happening anywhere else; certainly the Labour Party has never taken it fully on board. It is also essential to carry this into an international dimension by investigating what is happening in other countries, what questions are being posed and what creative new solutions are put forward. That is not to say that they should be copied, surely we have learned that lesson, but such information will widen our horizons. Only then will the left get beyond the provincialism of being rooted in one country and one national identity. And there is a final point. Contrasting ourselves with others can also help us understand how 'we' also contain diversity.

A RADICAL LEFT PROJECT?

Chantal Mouffe interviewed by Mike Power

Mike Power: How do ideas of radical democracy differ from those of liberalism and socialism? And how does it represent a new democratic idea for the 1990s? The left needs to be looking ahead and avoiding its old internecine political battles. But it needs to be clear about what is to replace some of its worn out ideological baggage.

Chantal Mouffe: First I want to insist that radical democracy does not require us to reject liberal democracy. It is important to distinguish between liberal democracy and capitalism. For too long the left has accepted the notion that the two necessarily go together. But we must show the difference between liberal democracy as a political form of society, as a regime which implies a specific mode of human coexistence, and capitalism. Some argue that so far we have only had capitalist liberal democracy, but there is not an essential link between the two and they can be separated. The project of radical democracy consists of struggling within the framework of liberal democracy in order to extend democratic principles to more and more social relations.

Perhaps a definition of liberal democracy would be helpful here.

Liberal democracy as a political form of society can also be referred to as modern pluralist democracy. It consists of the combination of two traditions. Firstly, political liberalism with its defence of individual rights, the rule of law and constitutional government. Secondly, the democratic tradition whose main ideas are equality and popular sovereignty. Its ethico-political principles are the assertion of liberty and equality for all. They inform the human mode of coexistence which is specific to liberal democracy. There is nothing wrong with these principles and I do not see how we could find any more radical principles on which to organise society. The problem is that they are not put into practice by societies that lay claim to them. This is why the left has usually seen them as a sham and declared that we have to destroy so-called 'bourgeois democracy' and work for the construction of a completely different society. This is precisely the kind of radical alternative that has been shown to be disastrous by the experience of Soviet-type socialism, which must be discarded.

Does that mean that we have to accept 'really existing capitalist liberal democracy' as the end of history?

No. There is still enormous potential for democratisation within the framework of liberal democracy; this society has to be made accountable for its ideals. And the project of radical and plural democracy is to radicalise those principles, not to seek other principles on which to establish another kind of society. The idea of revolution as a complete break therefore has to be abandoned, and the main reason is that we do not need such a break. We can realise the main objectives of socialism within a liberal democratic regime. Socialist goals must therefore be reinscribed within the framework of liberal democracy. Democracy should be conceived of as the struggle against all forms of autocratic power and socialism will be a specific dimension of that struggle.

In terms of the objectives of radical democracy, are you talking about finding a way in which to cut the links between the state and the people, or are you seeking to find new ways in which the people will influence the state?

One of the issues in the struggle for democracy where socialist goals are still relevant is the democratisation of private corporations, and of state administration. But that struggle must be waged in a way that respects the principles of liberal democracy.

You say, on one hand that we must abandon the idea of revolution as a complete break, but are you not actually proposing a revolutionary idea? And what are the specific socialist goals that should be reinscribed within liberal democracy?

If revolution means a change in the principles of the legitimacy of the regime, or a total break, then it has to be abandoned, because we do not need such a change. That is not to say that revolutionary change is not sometimes needed to establish the basis for the development of liberal democracy, like the overthrow of a dictatorship. But in the advanced western societies today we are seeking to radicalise an already existing liberal democracy. I find the idea of true democracy very dangerous because one of modern democracy's constructive ideas is pluralism, which does not come from the democratic tradition, but from the political liberal one. Pluralism means the respect for individual rights, expressed by John Stuart Mill as everybody having the right to choose their own ends, to their own way of life and to develop in their own way. It is linked to the ideas of toleration, the need to separate the state and religion, and the private and the public. These ideas do not come from the democratic but from the liberal tradition. For that reason liberalism is not something that we have to grudgingly accept, because it is absolutely central to the radical democratic project. Pluralism is the counterbalance to the tendency towards homogenisation, consensus and harmony, which can always emerge from the democratic tradition. Political modernity means the abandonment of the idea that there is one single common good that can be imposed on everybody, whether based on nature as in ancient societies, or on a religious vision, or on more recent democratic or communist ideas. Pluralism means that there are many different ways in which we can organise our lives, and this is what modern democracy must come to terms with. There is not a single unified homogeneous people.

We could therefore go through a period of struggle for radical democratic objectives, ideas and movements, and could develop new relations between people, including accepting the right of all to live how they choose. Could those struggles ultimately become sharp enough so that the essential nature of capitalism would change, although we will still not have undergone a revolution?

If in a liberal democratic regime there is a change in the economic organisation of society and it ceased to be capitalist this would not be a revolution. This would be a deep and profound transformation, but not a new regime. But we should be careful about terminology. Capitalism is not a monolithic system. There will not be a watershed, nor shall we will wake up one morning and find that capitalism is gone. We will probably always be dealing with a mixed economy. Britain, Sweden and the US are 'capitalist' countries, but have different forms of mixed economy. And the disastrous Soviet experiment showed that we cannot do without some market elements. While things like health and education should not be subject to the market, there are elements in the retail and wholesale sectors that work better privately. Even Marx never proposed the absolute nationalisation of everything. However, the market must not be the dominant logic, with all relations based on it. We must shift the balance towards more socially managed sectors, and accept that others will be run by the market. This brings us to the socialist goals within radical democracy. Socialist goals in themselves are not enough. They did not, for instance, include concern for relationships based on gender, race and sexuality. It is not merely a question of conflating or reformulating socialist ideas, and neither is it an abandonment of them. Socialism was formulated in the nineteenth century, and the issues mentioned are of more recent concern. The socialist input is relevant around the issues of democratisation of the economy and the state.

In 1977 the Communist Party of Great Britain (CPGB) developed its programme, the British Road to Socialism, which took into account the position of what it called the 'new social forces' and the way in which these forces could, as it were, be battened on to the class struggle and thereby challenge capitalism. How do you see that sort of approach? It took honest account of the new social forces and non-class areas of oppression. But why did that not work for us in the 1970s and 1980s? Was that because we attempted to impose it in a eurocommunist way rather than developing a radical democratic approach?

The attempts of the CPGB were certainly progressive and well intentioned and they were better than simply sticking to the traditional project. But it could not have worked because it was wrong to force the social movements concerned into the strait-jacket of socialism, and that is where the ideas of autonomy are important. The British Road to Socialism project was violating the specificity of those forces, but you were not the only ones doing it. The Labour left and Tony Benn were saying similar things about all these groups and called on them to join the Labour Party. This was not a promising strategy, because it coincided, for instance, with the attempts to explain women's exploitation through Marxism and show that there is only one solution to the relations of oppression. By contrast, radical democracy insists on the autonomy of the different movements that will work out different theories to explain different forms of subordination. What we need to do is link these expressions and struggles together and in that way create 'chains of equivalences' between these movements. It would not then be possible, for instance, to neutralise women's demands by shifting their burdens on to, say, immigrants. The theoretical idea behind this is hegemony. And the Gramscian background to that is important, because we cannot challenge an existing hegemony unless we articulate a counter hegemony. A single movement will not be able to profoundly transform the power relations in society because it faces a system of power which is based on a system of alliances. And here Thatcherism is a good example – it not only neutralised the democratic struggle by picking off separate groups but also coopted some aspects of it, what Gramsci called hegemony by neutralisation.

What is the agency for creating a chain of equivalences?

That is not a legitimate question. We should be very wary of the concept of agency. The left has always been seeking an agency for change whether it is the working class or new social movements. But it is now going to be very different historically and we need to establish different forms of articulation among democratic struggles and no one element of struggle should have a privileged position. At times one movement may play a more important role as a pole of attraction for struggle, but that would be a historic or cultural moment. As we are not seeking a 'revolutionary' change we do not need an 'agency'; we need a maximum number of struggles and their articulation.

If the chains of equivalence are to become hegemonic and impose change, are we not then in danger of radical democracy, which is theoretically informing that struggle, becoming a new universal idea?

No, because radical democracy is not a model of society. It is a non-ending process, because, paradoxically, if democracy could ever be realised it would self-destruct. It is a self refuting idea. How can we have a perfectly democratic society? It would mean that there is no more possibility of challenge and people would be expected to be happy with their lot. That would not be democratic or pluralist. Radical democracy is a struggle for radicalising the principles of liberty and equality for all by extending them to more and more social relations. But there will always be a struggle for the interpretation of those principles and the type of social relations that would apply. Radical democracy is one interpretation of those principles. It goes beyond the restricted liberal interpretation, which exists only within the political arena and highlights the equality of the vote. A social democratic interpretation extends those principles further within society, but radical democracy wants to go beyond areas like the economy and extend them to all relations where any form of inequality and subordination exists. Such an extension will be different in each society and it cannot therefore be a universal model. It is a form of democratic politics which is historically specific, and can only start with organised movements and actual relations. It can never be imposed.

Democratic Left is talking about how it may transform itself out of an old-time socialist/communist way of doing things. Democratic centralism has gone along with Marxism-Leninism and we have replaced this with feminism, anti-racism, environmentalism and a creative Marxism. Our major areas of concern include, along with the above, youth, lesbians and gays and peace and we are seeking to engage with these struggles. The organisation is however facing a crisis because although these ideas are those of the 1990s, it still has, to paraphrase Marx, carried with it the birthmarks of the old party. So how can we develop these radical democratic ideas? We are not a single issue movement but seek to network with others in struggle and engage with them. How do you think our members and resources, who have a clear identification with these struggles, be best used? If we do not clarify this we could degenerate into a politics of moral outrage.

This question calls to mind the experience of the New American Movement (NAM) of the 1970s which later became the Democratic Socialists of America. One requirement for members of NAM was to be involved in a concrete struggle, and their political role was not to recruit them, but to take some political consciousness to those movements and help to make people aware of each other's common struggles. They were involved in single issue movements, which they saw as sacrosanct, but aimed to break out of the single issue framework. But for Democratic Left and its practical application there is one specific idea that should be central to your work, and that is pluralism. It is important to bring valid socialist goals into radical democratic struggle as well as rapidly advancing the transformation that you have gone through by progressing those areas of struggle that you enumerated. It is important to show that far from being in contradiction with the principles of liberal democracy, that the socialist tradition of thought can help to enrich and deepen its pluralist objectives. It could, for instance, contribute to the formulation of a new approach to individuality that highlights its social nature and stresses the crucial role of citizenship, understood as belonging to the political community.

Pluralism may be a challenge to the state but it also challenges the old-fashioned centralist organisations of the left. Will an advance of pluralist ideas inspired by radical democracy help, for instance, to break the statist relationship between the trade unions and the Labour Party and bring the unions back into civil society where they may develop a much more pluralistic relationship with their members?

Such a break would be extremely positive. Union activity should be more diversified and less dependent on their state and party links. They should aim to be much more involved in community provision of things like health, education and cultural pursuits. In some countries unions are even open to non-members, which helps the unemployed. But you use the term civil society too loosely. It is not just a case of civil society being good and the state bad. We need a different form of interaction between them. For example, in many feminist struggles we need the state to fight against sexism in civil society, which contains sexist, as well as racist and many other forms of oppression. The state must be democratised, pluralised and made less bureaucratic, but it is not the only centre where relations of domination exist. We need 'public spaces' within the state. And the key issue is that of accountability.

Finally, is there any way in which a creative Marxist element can

be identified within the radical democratic project? Or is it a post-Marxist idea?

It is certainly post-Marxist in both senses as we emphasised in *Hegemony and Socialist Strategy* (London: Verso, 1985). It is 'post' in the sense that it goes further. But it is not post-Marxist in the sense of an abandonment or renunciation of the tradition. It draws on the Gramscian tradition of hegemony and this is the crucial connection, although the project goes much further than Gramsci. However, the project could have been formulated without Marxism. I have personally come to it through Marxism and my work on Gramsci, but this is not essential and it could unite people from many traditions.

DEMOCRACY BY INSTALMENTS

Ernesto Laclau interviewed by Adam Lent

Adam Lent: Following the collapse of the traditional ideological options of the twentieth century, why do you feel radical democracy is now particularly relevant? In your work you seem to provide explanations which operate both at the level of the sociological (e.g. disorganised capitalism, social fragmentation) and the philosophical (e.g. contemporary approaches to the human subject). Could you outline both explanations and their links?

Ernesto Laclau: I would not speak of two types of explanations but of one type of explanation, some dimensions of which have been traditionally dealt with in the sociological literature, while others have received a more philosophical treatment. For example the category of 'social dislocation' (the situation in which accepted values and identities are brought into question by a major change in human relations, for example, the destruction of rural communities in the fifteenth and sixteenth centuries) which is central to my approach to the pattern that social struggles follow in the contemporary world. At a merely descriptive level the explanation of social dislocations could seem sociological, but as soon as you try to come to terms with what is involved in a relation of dislocation you enter into a terrain which is beyond anything that any sociological explanation can offer. This question of the proliferation of social dislocations in the contemporary world gives us also a starting point to approach your first question concerning the relevance of radical democracy as a political option for our age. Radical democracy is conceived as the radicalisation of the democratic revolution – a process which started with the emergence of egalitarianism at the time of the French revolution, and consequently spread to wider areas of social relations such as the economy, relations between the sexes, and ethnic and national groups. Now, this spread is more difficult in relatively stable societies, in which traditional hierarchical forms of social organisation prevail. But the dislocations that are, among other things, the result of modern capitalism, require a constant reconstitution of social identities along new lines; new groups and new demands are launched into the historical arena which can be radicalised around egalitarian ideals, and this gives radical democracy its chance. Only a chance, however, because we know very well that such radicalisation can go in many directions that are not democratic at all. These more complex relations between social identities explain the need for more subtle theoretical instruments than those which were at hand for Marxism or for classical sociology.

How do you avoid radical democracy becoming an explain-all ideology? One could imagine an argument being formed that pluralism – a central principle of your formulation of radical democracy – is somehow inherent to human nature and as such an abuse against pluralism becomes stigmatised as a crime against the whole of humanity itself. Thus radical democracy runs the risk of speaking on behalf of the whole of the human race in just the very way you say political outlooks should avoid. I say this partly because Chantal Mouffe, with whom you have written, has said she welcomes people from other traditions working around the notion of radical democracy. But these traditions might not share your awareness of the dangers of creating explain-all ideologies?

Radical democracy is not an ideology. It is just a general principle. If you try to turn it into a blueprint of society, there will always come a point where you do not want to extend democracy any further – there will be people who you will want to exclude. So radical democracy is not an explain-all ideology, it is a logic by which we can construct the social. From this point of view, I do not think that the first danger that you point out – that pluralism becomes something attributed to human nature and a new universalism – does even arise. Pluralism arises, on the contrary, from the recognition that there is no human nature, that different cultures and perspectives are incompatible with each other, and that, as a result, political formulae have to be found that make possible the coexistence of these incompatible identities, formulae which cannot pass through any form of authoritarian unification. If the incompatibility becomes a reason for exclusion there is no longer the possibility of a democratic community. And the examples of these exclusionary particularisms are obvious, from Lebanon to Yugoslavia. The reason for my cautious optimism vis-a-vis this obvious danger is linked to the profoundly fragmented nature of contemporary societies. If an ethnic or national minority attempts to assert itself in a world or community larger than itself, it will have to do so in terms of principles that are more universal than itself – that is the right of nations or cultural groups to their self-determination. This can create a new universalism, which does not emerge from any 'universal class' but which is precisely linked to the affirmation of pluralism and difference.

Do you see radical democracy growing 'naturally' out of a plurality of loosely connected, or even totally unconnected, struggles or do you feel that, at some point, it is necessary for those struggles to unite under the banner of radical democracy as though it were a unifying principle?

Radical democracy certainly does not necessarily grow out of a plurality of unconnected social struggles, for nothing guarantees that these struggles coalesce harmoniously with each other. Even more each struggle can be constructed in ways which are incompatible with each other. Their possible unification can only be the result of a process of complex political construction. There are two important points. The first is that there is no question of a political unification of the various social struggles. Each of them operates in areas which are specific to them and their unification would only lead to bureaucratic authoritarianism. But if we speak of 'radical democracy' we speak of a type of relation different from political unification: we speak of a certain democratic culture in which a plurality of social struggles are perceived and lived as belonging to the same family. This is certainly a hegemonic formation, but the idea of a hegemonic or unifying principle that you introduce forces me to introduce a further classification, which is my second point. A hegemonic formation is not unified by a principle that can be defined in terms of precise contents, such as 'socialism'. From this point of view, each social demand belonging to that formation contributes equally to the constitution of that principle. In that sense, as hegemony is an open process in which new demands are constantly incorporated, the verifying principle has to be subject to constant redefinitions – it is, to use a technical term, a 'floating signifier'.

Some writers, such as Roberto Unger, have tried to develop a vision of the actual features that might belong to a radical democratic society. Even though you are against detailed blueprints, are there, nevertheless, clear social features of a radical democracy? I ask this partly because radical democracy has been criticised for possessing the very character you give it, of just being a principle and thus being too vague.

I wish it was still vaguer because that would mean that its social effectiveness would be higher. I think the problem is the following. We have to distinguish between a political programme, which is a set of concrete but changing proposals and an imaginary horizon which is made up of visions and values that mould the whole approach of a varied group of social forces. 'Communism', for instance, or 'moral majority' are from this point of view social imaginaries: they express global attitudes which cannot be reduced to one specific set of concrete political proposals. For many decades, 'communism' represented for vast masses over the world, not simply an economic formula linked to the social management of the means of production, but the promise of a remedy to all forms of social injustice, a horizon into which all grievances and social demands could be inscribed. 'Moral majority' plays the same role for conservative forces. If an imaginary horizon is going to play this role it has to be necessarily vague and transcend all concrete political programmes. 'Radical democracy' as the extension of the principle of equality to wider social spheres, attempts to be a social imaginary. I firmly believe that the present crisis of the left is not so much linked to the failure of concrete policies, but rather to the fact that both communism and social democracy, the two classical imaginary horizons of the left, have ceased to galvanise the imagination of the masses and are no longer viable languages for the expression of radical social demands.

Radical Democracy has also been accused of being Eurocentric, that it is based upon principles that only have a meaning in the West and have no resonance in the Third World. Do you regard this as a genuine problem?

No, to a large extent the opposite is true. Political alternatives in the Third World take less and less the form of unified and centralised political movements of the type which followed the processes of decolonisation. What we are witnessing in the Third World today is a process of social fragmentation intimately linked to the marginalisation of vast sections of the population. In Latin America, for instance, social struggles take place less around attempts to impose global solutions, and increasingly around specific demands of local groups. If we link radical democracy to the social demands arising from fragmented constituencies, this is increasingly the situation in the Third World. Multiculturalism, which is such a big issue in America today, has always been characteristic of the Third World. Post-modernity itself actually started in the Third World. There never were there the highly efficient state apparatuses which could absorb a plurality of social demands. So the phenomena of fragmentation and disorganised capitalism which are, in the West, approached as characteristic of postmodernity, have always been present in the Third World.

That is very interesting because many of the critics of post-modernism argued that examples of post modernism such as postFordist styles of factory production, were something that applied solely to the West. Mike Rustin said that although there had been post-Fordist changes in the West, a far more important trend was the export of traditional Fordist production processes to the Third World.

Something of that is true, although it is far from being as general a trend as Rustin thinks. But I think it irrelevant for the discussion concerning post-modernity. What is characteristic of the latter is not so much the predominance of one or another style of production, but a process of social fragmentation that turns obsolete the forms of social and state control that had been typical of modernity. Now, the existence, in Third World countries, of poles of high development and social marginalisation, which increase the combined and uneven development of those societies, creates a postmodern situation before any 'modernity' could be constituted. And given the current trends of world capitalism, this situation is irreversible: whatever the future of Third World societies, it will not pass through the forms of social and state organisation which have been characteristic of modernity in the West.

Chantal Mouffe has said that radical democracy is not a revolutionary politics because it does not aim to change the principle by which Liberal democracies gain their legitimacy – that is, accountability and the democratic process. But this does not seem a full explanation: although liberal democracies may, in theory, gain their legitimacy through democratic processes, we have, in practice, seen an increasing reliance on coercion as a way of dealing with dissent, especially in the last 15 years – for example, the miners' strike. So could it be said that radical democracy is revolutionary precisely because it tries to reimpose the grand principles of liberal democracies that seem to have been forgotten by those systems that call themselves liberal-democratic?

Everything depends on what we understand by 'revolutionary'. You are certainly right in saying that to reimpose the grand principles of liberal democracies would require drastic changes which would involve protracted struggles and major upheavals. I also agree with you that in some cases there has been an increasing tendency to resort to coercion to deal with dissent in the West – although I do not think that we can speak here of a general trend. French society, for instance, has become considerably less repressive over the last 10 years. But this is not the sense of 'revolutionary' that Chantal was using. What she was referring to was 'revolution' in the sense of a Jacobin break, of a radical change of the political regime (a sense of revolution that the Marxist tradition shared with Jacobinism). And it is clear that no change of this type is envisaged by a radical democratic view of the liberal state. We are not thinking about the establishment of a one party system, or eliminating elections, freedom of the press or the division of powers. Radical democracy is a change within the liberal state, not a radical alternative to the latter.

THE PARTY'S OVER

Geoff Mulgan interviewed by Noni Stacey

Noni Stacey: Why did you decide to create Demos, a think tank, rather than work within existing political structures?

Geoff Mulgan: Demos evolved from an analysis of political systems and the way in which parties are locked into those systems. There is growing evidence that the core political system of parties and parliaments is gradually losing its capacity to generate social solutions to problems, to be legitimate, and to reflect the aspirations and fears of ordinary people. In Italy, for example, the strength of the Lombard League, in contrast to the weakness of the Party of the Democratic Left on one side and the Christian Democrats on the other is part of the political crisis. It translates itself into a move towards electoral reform and the adoption of a first-past-the-post electoral system. In France it is reflected in the decline of core political parties on both left and right, the strength of the Greens, the National Front and widespread anti-political feeling. In America, Ross Perot was a conduit for political disillusion whereas in Britain it is evident in a sullen lack of faith that politicians and parties hold answers to everyday problems. The root causes of the long-term decay of our political system stem from the changing role and credibility of states, and their waning power in a more internationalised economy but also the development of the party system based on the nineteenth century ideologies – conservatism, liberalism and socialism. These ideological traditions have proven themselves less able to generate innovative and pertinent solutions.

Is the party political system therefore able to generate any radical ideas?

Political parties are not able to generate either radical or even less conservative ideas. Faced with persistent unemployment, threats to the environment and problems of national security the political world is much less credible in its attempts to identify problems and seek solutions than it was in the nineteenth century. Despite the new wave of political issues that emerged over 20 years ago, racial, Green and women's issues have not been integrated into political systems. That is why a new kind of political institution is needed, which fosters radical political thought but avoids locking itself organically into existing parties or ideological structures. To do so would be the kiss of death to correct analysis, originality or to striking a chord with a wider public.

What about the trade unions? Do you see them as having any future?

On balance the unions are in slow decline. However, in the short run, partly because of the dramatic weakness of central government, they seem to have become more important. This can be seen because the government is talking to them again. The unions' weight in society is nevertheless in long-term decline. Unions are weaker in the sectors of the future, where employment outstrips the declining sectors. This will determine whether or not unions are a materially important force. However, the worst could be over. Unions have taken some ideas from business, and are offering members services such as credit cards and insurance schemes. What they have not done is become membership-driven organisations. But this should be their unique selling point and distinctive role. They should not simply provide services that the private sector can make available more efficiently. The unions should now be debating their reinvention and how to strategically position themselves to become important institutions in 10 to 20 years time. But they will never again be as important as they once were.

Let us now look at where Demos stands in relation to the Institute of Public Policy and Research (IPPR), the Labour Coordinating Committee (LCC) and Democratic Left (DL)? Does this herald the formation of a new political grouping?

Demos is different in that it is not a faction. IPPR is a Labour Party think tank. LCC and DL are in a traditional sense parties or factions within parties which have a programme and which, according to the logic of such institutions, see their role as winning power, either within a party or within the nation, in order to exercise power and implement a programme. Demos includes

Tories, Liberals and people who are not politically affiliated. A think tank is able to operate in a much more open-minded, catholic and creative way, though it runs the risk of not always being consistent or coherent. Demos does not require a consensus of opinion or dogged adherence to a political line, in fact the aim is to operate in the opposite way.

How will Demos' ideas be integrated into political debate?

It is a question of gradually building a series of recurrent, informing themes, derived from both ethics and ideology, which will shape the way in which Demos will react to problems. It is a question of relationships as opposed to the old dichotomy between state and market or the division between collectives and individuals. Contemporary political issues revolve around relationships and the qualities of those relationships within a company or voluntary organisation, between government and citizens, or a service like the NHS, its doctors, nurses, patients and the outside community. Demos aims to work with practitioners working in hospitals, schools, companies or consultancies and the legal system, as well as with theorists, academics, think tanks and journalists. Wherever possible, the aim is to make practitioners the bearers of these ideas, rather than expecting the political system at the top of these structures to be the force for change. Demos will, however, retain close contact with politicians and political organisations.

Which issues is Demos tackling first?

Europe is not high on our agenda at the moment. Demos is assembling a group to shape an agenda for the 1996 inter-government conference. The issues dominating the European agenda are ones of collective security, of protection from a whole series of threats, for example the inflows of people or persistent wars on the borders of the EC. The present period focusing on questions of monetary union may be drawing to a close on the battlefields of Serbia and the dole queues of EC member states. The single most important collective security issue may be the environment. It is patently absurd that this be managed at a national level.

How will the response to these questions be coordinated on a international level?

The EC is taking on powers in the environmental field, by policing the actions of member states, to try to force through common environmental tax policies such as carbon taxes. The British government is making the case that the principle of subsidiarity requires environmental regulation be handled at a national level. It is hard to see the logic of that. There is clearly immense resistance around moving such powers upwards, even to an EC level and beyond that to a global level, witness the relative failure of the Earth Summit.

How will Demos approach the issues of tax and electoral reform?

Demos is examining the relationship between tax and the democratic process, rather than electoral reform as a stand-alone issue. It is more interested in how, in a mature democracy, citizens can have a greater choice and responsibility for spending decisions. At the moment, it is still assumed that every four or five years citizens are required to vote between two or three parties offering a package of policies, with almost no room for picking and choosing between them. The current electoral system and the reforms under consideration by electoral reform organisations will not increase the richness of choice given to citizens. Demos is examining ways of giving the electorate choices over spending levels, particularly in core services of health and education, and of returning control over tax and spending to local communities.

This requires a widespread realignment of powers – how long will this take?

This type of agenda will start happening very quickly because at the moment governments are stuck in an extraordinary impasse – no government dares to raise taxes. Left-wing parties which promise to raise taxes tend to get defeated at the polls. At the same time, governments are visibly constrained in terms of cutting public spending. Some of these methods of democratising the tax process may solve a problem for governments, in that the voter will determine the level of health or education spending.

How does this tie in with a revival in the ethic of social responsibility?

This is something which has been missing from the democratic and left traditions in this country and elsewhere: how to encourage people and communities to take responsibility for their own lives. The political culture has been about how government solves problems for people and takes responsibility away from them. One alternative is to offer tax payers the opportunity to opt in or out of taxes which target specific problems.

Do you believe people will choose to opt in?

How can you know? There are a great many ways in which one could experiment with testing out people's commitment to the community. Traditionally the response has been one of not trusting people to take that sort of decision, for fear they will make the wrong decision. When you get into a persistent culture of not trusting people, either electorates or communities, that distrust tends to become mutual. Demos will publish a pamphlet on tax to launch a research project on the different dimensions of tax, including new subscription tax models, local opt-in and opt-out models, the taxation of business and the institutional relationship between the Inland Revenue and the DSS.

Who is involved with Demos?

The core group includes myself, Martin Jacques, Julia Middleton of Common Purpose, and Bob Tyrell of the Henley Centre. Demos has deliberately chosen not to have politicians formally involved on councils or committees, but we have links with MPs in all parties. Many younger, brighter MPs from all parties are aware of the deficiencies of both their organisations and the role of the politician.

Can Demos put a timescale on its work?

There is a series of timescales. Some publications will aim to have an immediate impact and generate a lively debate, preferably beyond the normal circles of political argument. It is hoped that some of these ideas will be absorbed into policy, if not the policy of national government, then the policy of local government, voluntary organisations, trade unions, or companies. Other work though will be long-term in effect. There are two parallells, the Institute of Economic Affairs (IEA) and the Fabian Society. The Fabians only really started influencing national policy after 20 or 30 years. The IEA, set up in the 1950s, developed much of the political agenda of the 1980s. Hopefully Demos will not have that sort of timescale, but it is important that Demos resists pressures to respond to the short-term or even medium-term political necessities of parties needing programmes or governments needing solutions to problems. Those think tanks which were prepared to burrow down a bit and think longer-term and reach the fundamental nature of issues were much more useful and productive in the long run.

What would be the most favourable outcome for Demos – and the most disappointing?

Demos wants to be a catalyst for shifting culture, introducing a set of new ideas, and rethinking the way politics is considered. Demos will consider itself successful if more people feel comfortable with political debate that is open-minded and less partisan, and if the disillusionment and contempt for orthodox politics endemic in those under 30 years old can be channelled in a more positive direction. If Demos can reverse this demoralisation and return to the old idea that the world is malleable, and not simply inherited, it will have succeeded. I would not want to measure our success by the number of policies which are implemented by national government, important though that is. There are two dangers: one is that Demos is mistaken about the political changes and the capacity of political parties for regeneration, or for inspiring people and solving problems. In that case Demos will not be a relevant or important institution. This is not a major worry. The second is that the project is five or 10 years ahead of its time and that people will be confused because it is too far ahead of history. It will be hard organisationally to keep coherence until the time is right. There may be a danger of trying to hit too many targets at once and of losing a degree of coherence. This is not a worry, so long as it is a creative process, rather than diversity for its own sake.

Who will have access to Demos events?

Discussion groups will number between eight to 10 people as groups of this size tend to provide the best sort of discussions and learning processes. Participants will be chosen carefully to try to establish a balance between theoretical people and practitioners. Outsiders will also be included. With healthcare, for example, someone who has no professional knowledge of healthcare except as a patient will be included, providing added insights which come from not knowing much about the policy debates. It is not a membership organisation but subscribers will receive our publications.

PART FIVE

TOWARDS TRANSFORMATION:
THE NEARLY NEW POLITICS OF THE 1990S

The Earth's Rocky Road from Rio

Jonathon Porritt interviewed by **Quentin Given**

Quentin Given: You said of the Rio summit that your lowest expectations had been fulfilled. Is anything buried in the paper-work of Rio going to feed through into any real change?

Jonathon Porritt: They will feed through, but you can't expect instant changes as a result. For instance, the decision to create a UN Commission for Sustainable Development won't be approved until the General Assembly in November 1993 and it won't really be into its stride for another two years. So it's difficult to say that things are going to happen immediately, but there is no doubt that the decisions create a process which allows for considerable improvement in international policy in the critical areas of climate change, biological diversity and sustainable development. So I'm not surprised that we have the same flood of idiotic, earth-bashing decisions that we had before the summit. It takes a long time to educate politicians who've spent their entire lives engaged in a process that destroys the world so they can see for themselves how alternatives will begin to work. There's no short cut to these things.

Some people say it's not the agreements that matter but the beginning of a new consciousness involving world leaders and the business community. Is there evidence of that consciousness?

Yes. It was very interesting, if one could actually stomach it, to watch the world leaders delivering their seven minutes worth of Green strategies! The challenge for politicians today, of managing human aspirations on a finite and rapidly degrading planet, is a massively complex one. There are very few people who've got the leadership skills to articulate that to the people. Having spent decades persuading everybody that the best means of progress is producing and consuming more, they now suddenly realise they've got to find alternatives to that. This is tricky stuff. It was deeply ironic that the only world leader who got a rousing cheer at the end of his speech was Fidel Castro, and he offered no particular vision for the future but actually said some home truths about the idiocy of capitalism attempting to address the problems according to its current lights.

It was said before the summit that John Major wasn't particularly interested in the environment. But Major also announced some new initiatives over the period of the summit . Is that just window dressing or is this government going to take a lead on environmental issues?

It's still very much in the balance. I think John Major is discovering the importance of environmental issues. It was interesting that as soon as he got back to London after the summit , he wrote a letter to other G7 leaders saying we've now got to start to deliver on these things, for instance we've got to produce action plans as to how we intend to reduce or stabilise carbon dioxide emissions by the year 2000. Whatever else he may be, one gets the very strong feeling that John Major is a man of principle, and I believe that once he has subscribed to a series of principled positions on environmental matters, then he will seek to do something about them. By all accounts he enjoyed being in Rio; he found it fascinating and very challenging. The one thing about the Earth summit is that politicians' noses were rubbed in the reality of ecological degradation. And that is helpful.

Environmental issues have now been forced onto the agenda of large businesses. In the world of big business is there any deep shift in priorities going on that is strong enough to counter short-term profit motives?

Not strong enough to counter short-term profit motives, no. Because the laws of that world are utterly ruthless – if you are not increasing short term profitability then you won't be in business. So there isn't much choice for them on that score, and although they can temper the damage done, and seek to make profit out of less damaging activities or products, by and large the nature of their activities must remain the same, which is to maximise productivity and increase turnover. In the long term, that is completely incompatible with sustainable development.

That is not to say that the business community isn't genuinely beginning to grapple with these issues. Companies have realised that this is no longer a public relations issue. It is now a matter of their long-term success as to whether or not they succeed in meeting the challenge better than their competitors. Companies are made up of people who care about their children, probably care about their environment and maybe even care about things like the Third World as much as some people in other occupations do. I hope we'll find ways of working with the business community a bit more amicably. That doesn't mean we stop criticising them, or stop pointing out that the world's 25 largest multinational companies are now responsible for the vast amount of damage being done. It's a more sophisticated game for the Green movement than we were once accustomed to playing.

In the longer term, is achieving a sustainable economy on a global scale compatible with the existing structures we have?

No. What I think we face is a clear opportunity to push hard on areas of policy convergence between good environmental practice and good commercial practice. On all of the easy things – like waste minimisation, energy efficiency, proper use of resources, recycling – there is an area of convergence ahead of us which we haven't even begun to fill. And that can be done more or less within the confines of the existing economy. But if we're talking about meeting the needs of 10 or 11 billion people in a sustainable manner, any economy that is premised upon the expansion of economic activity as an end in itself cannot meet the challenge of sustainability because it's just logically impossible to do it. So at that point one has to talk about different patterns of work creation, in which we look much more at production of what, for what benefit, what kind of growth we can afford and what kind of growth would be beneficial, and we need to look much more at the distribution of the proceeds of that wealth creation to ensure sustainability. You can't have a sustainable society where you've got a rich elite of the sort that we have, and an emerging underclass of the sort that we're going to have in a very short time, and say, 'Yes, we're really into sustainable development' – really? One has to ram those messages home time after time.

How do you see that change coming about? The results of elections, in this country and elsewhere, don't show a move in that direction – if anything, the reverse.

Inevitably the consequences of continuing as we do now will need to impinge on people more painfully before the arguments for change become sufficiently convincing. To that extent I agree that things are likely to get worse before they get better, and I mean both ecologically and socially. But I think there is already a readiness to accept the need for a change in terms of the shape of our economy, and a tremendous readiness, although it wasn't reflected in the 1992 General Election, to move towards a society in which humane, compassionate and sharing cooperative values are given far more space than they are in current society. I have to say though that the opposition seems to be hardly capable of articulating those values. People continue to underestimate the scale of the challenge that we're talking about, not just in terms of dealing with powerful vested interests, but the extent to which they're capable of manipulating media, images, advertising etc. We're talking about a historical process that started with the industrial revolution: about generations of indoctrination about how we should meet human needs and what the nature of a successful economy is. Anybody who thinks they can turn that round in one or two elections needs to think again. It will take generations to reverse a set of values which have been demonstrated as wholly immoral and unsustainable.

In an article in the June 1992 BBC *Wildlife* magazine you criticised the environmental movement for allowing the two main parties and the media to ignore Green issues throughout the election campaign, and failing to mobilise public anger and fear in the approach to the Earth summit. You contrasted Charter 88's imaginative intervention on the issue of democracy. Is that just a problem for Friends of the Earth?

I think it's a very wide problem, that affects all environmental organisations. I hope it will lead to a re-evaluation about what we're trying to do in the Green movement and the ways in which we should do it. When things were going well for the environment movement, members and money were flowing in, the media were listening, the politicians were at least pretending to listen, and it absolved those organisations from serious strategic analysis. At the moment the Green movement is winning the real support of, let's be optimistic, say 15 per cent of the population. We're not going to do anything until we've got 75 per cent. So how are we going to reach out to those new constituencies, how are we going to work through local community groups, women's groups, church groups, the business community?

The second thing – and if it isn't obvious now then it never will be – is that dealing with environmental problems as environmental problems is worthless. We're talking now about problems that always go back to the economy, so until we develop enormous economic expertise within the Green movement, we'll miss the point. We shouldn't be appointing any more environmental campaigners, we should be appointing and training scores of economists to deal with issues at that level!

Thirdly, and the public are going to demand this whether we like it or not – how do we learn to work better together? How do we find processes of cooperation, active and passive networking, which will avoid the duplication that still goes on and will give a concerted, clear image of what priorities we stand for? How are we going to prioritise activities? Is a frog tunnel as important as eliminating CFCs? The problem is a real one that we cannot leave simply to the process of media advocacy. The Green movement at the moment has become too policy oriented. They devote too much time to lobbying government at the expense of increasing awareness and building new support which will give political momentum to those policy changes.

Is this just a British phenomenon?

I think that in some countries one can still generate a kind of raw political energy which can be locked into a broad sustainability agenda. Apart from WWF (World Wide Fund for Nature), which did attempt to get their existing supporters to understand what it was about, the other environment groups treated the Earth summit like just another environment conference. No efforts were made to explain what the issues were, what we thought should be going on, or to work together to make damn certain the Government knew what we thought. So there was no popular initiative based around the Earth summit. This made the whole process incredibly elitist with different experts hacking away at wording issues and amending documents and square brackets in Rio declarations – totally irrelevant to 99.9 per cent of people in this country. I don't know whether that elitism is a specific UK phenomenon, but I know the history of the UK environmental movement means that it can occasionally allow the gap between policy development work and awareness building to get too great. And when that gap reaches the point when it's only the specialists in the environment groups who understand why certain issues are so important, and nobody back here understands that the issue even exists, then we're in trouble. Over the last two years we've seen a widening of that gap, which has now to be filled.

Is some ferment now going on within the environmental movement?

So I gather on the grapevine, yes.

How can we help get the process moving faster?

It's up to the membership of every organisation never to let its representatives, or the people who work for it, become complacent or unthinking. I'm not accusing any of the groups of irresponsibility or waste of resources or arrogance, but I'm not sure they're doing their job with enough forethought. You can't go on doing something just because that's what you've always done. We live in a world that is changing rapidly. I hope members and local groups would be vocal in putting pressure on their organisations to take account of these new factors.

What do you think your own contribution is going to be over the next few years?

Well I'm still thinking about what the next steps are going to be. I shall continue writing and lecturing, a bit of broadcasting, freelance campaigning work – supporting smaller organisations. I shall remain very involved with campaigns like Oxleas Wood because they matter enormously to me. I've got various thoughts about what we should be doing politically for the next the next election, which I'm going to be exploring, and I'm also very interested in trying to pursue my own particular obsession with promoting good news. If all people ever hear is just the litany of dreadful threats and warnings, what is there to motivate people? What sense of joy, of excitement, of challenge, of service to others are we giving people?

What all that means in the longer term, I've no idea. I'm not likely to be doing it actively through the Green Party. I shall remain a member for as long as I am able to do so – but what happens to the Green Party is itself a bit of a mystery. I'm not likely to be joining another political party, but I am likely to be seeking ways of bringing together people who share a similar sense of values, as well as policies, and seeing how we can promote that before the next election. This is a time of enormous intellectual excitement – the shape of it, the outline of it is there now, in the public domain. The business of how we marry together different agendas to find the common ground and work together is intensely exciting – let a thousand green poppies bloom!

Troubled Pleasure

Kate Soper interviewed by **Anne Coddington**

Anne Coddington: In your book *Troubled Pleasures* (London: Verso, 1990) you talk about the need to disturb rather than abandon ideas of socialism despite the unacceptable connotations which rise from the Eastern Europe example and the centralised undemocratic principles of state welfarism. Instead you say socialism should be redefined to take into account ecological questions and advocate a less production orientated idea of the good life, and express an alternative and compelling vision that provides a pleasing prospect but without irresponsible levels of consumption. How will this approach contribute to a more positive socialist politics?

Kate Soper: It is ironic that the question of the future of socialism is only being addressed seriously following the collapse of an order in Eastern Europe which most socialists in the West have regarded as a travesty of socialism. It is as if we were unconsciously linking the prospects of socialism to the staying power of actually existing socialism even as we were consciously rejecting that model. Only now are we recognising how important it is to the future of socialism that we spell out the form of society – the authentic socialism – which we opposed to the Soviet model. Doing this today may involve rethinking the arguments used to recommend the socialist alternative. These have been two-fold. First, there has been an appeal to the self interest of the working class and what it would gain from a socialist society in directly material ways. Secondly it has based its case for egalitarianism on a broader and more altruistic appeal to a human sense of social justice. In the event, those who stood to gain most materially have prospered sufficiently under capitalism to make the socialist alternative less dramatically compelling. Equally a concern for social justice has not proved enough in itself to persuade people that a shift is necessary. This means the prospects for socialism today must be linked to the capacity of the left to project an alternative vision that is both practically convincing and attractive, in that it represents the possibility of enjoying goods which capitalism is incapable of delivering.

Socialism has to look both institutionally feasible and seductive – and seductive in part because of what everyone can hope to gain from it. This means enticing people with a vision of the good life which promises more pleasure and security than that associated with conventional politics and its goal of constantly increased material standards of living. People are not likely to make transformations in their own forms of consumption and rethink the question of affluence simply because of moral appeals about ecological attrition, the north-south divide or famine in Africa, although there is real concern about these issues, unless they are persuaded that there is an alternative order which is both workable and enjoyable.

The socialist appeal today must then be to a differently conceived notion of self interest and the good life. It should win people to the idea that a more sober and eco-friendly level of materialist consumption would allow them to be more widely profligate in their enjoyment of other gratifications such as more space, free time or a healthier environment – a whole range of dimensions of living that bring pleasures that cannot be valued in monetary terms and which we have scarcely begun to imagine. But in considering the prospects for socialism it would be a mistake to put all the emphasis on the blueprinting exercise needed. We can also point to popular disillusionment with untrammelled capitalism as evidence of potential support for an alternative. Moreover, what is really going for socialism is the greater rationality of its response to ecological crisis. Capitalism is on a collision course with the growing global requirement to accommodate environmental degradation and if left to itself will accentuate social divisions, nationally and internationally to catastrophic proportions.

Socialism would allow for a redistribution of resources and a more egalitarian consciousness nationally and globally. It is the only kind of planning of the economy and use of resources that, in breaking with the logic of the market, allows us to think about organising different working patterns. The market logic is resource hungry whereas socialism could in principle cut back on production in ways that would allow part-time work and a more eco-friendly conception of consumption and production. But just because socialism is the more rational solution does not mean that it is guaranteed to command popular support.

How can a socialist formation convince people that alternative ways of living can bring different but equally important pleasures?

Imagination. One role of social movements is to be very imaginative, to project non puritanical forms of what our pleasures could be. Maybe the left should be thinking of more carnivalesque types of campaigning and put more energy into envisaging an alternative utopian project. This might involve rethinking what we mean by a materialist consumption, in ways which highlight the amount of time and resources we invest in the production of sanitised commodities which in fact distance us from a more immediately sensual experience: the motor car, for example, has structured both urban and rural space in ways which limit our forms of access to it, and deny the sensory pleasures it might otherwise afford. What we call 'material' consumption is here directly at odds with physical gratification.

Given that there has been a mood swing in politics towards the celebration of individuality and diversity, the notion of class as a vehicle for socialist transformation is unlikely to resonate with people's experiences or desires. What will the agent of transformation be?

This is a difficult question. Socialism has in its orthodox form been too closely associated with class politics. The focus on class exploitation and the isolation of the working class as the sole agent of revolutionary change led to the other issues of race, gender, peace and ecology being tacked on as a laundry list of items to an essentialist socialist core. This is already being revised in socialist politics. The new social movements have here acted as an agent in changing popular perceptions, if only fairly marginally. They are important in bringing about a slow and gradual transformation in values, even if they cannot act as a directly effective political power for change. Ideally a radical alternative politics should work in conjunction with a political party so it can be put before the public more effectively and eventually seek a mandate for its programme. It is unfortunate that the Labour Party did not conceive itself as an agency of this kind at the beginning of the Thatcherite period, when there was an enormous amount of energy in social movement politics begging for the Labour Party to take it on. Had it done so, it could have gone through the Thatcher years consolidating a strong ideological alternative to the Tories and might now be in a better standing with the public.

As you point out, it is one thing to be aware that the way we live is irrational but it is another to actually change things given that we are are tied into the capitalist system. For example the hospital workers may recognise that hospital closures and moves to a system of primary care would be more cost effective and efficient but the resulting job losses will force them into opposition out of self interest. How can this tension be overcome?

We are trapped in the capitalist market for primary goods and it is difficult to see how to get out of a dependency on capital investment for the provisioning of pensions and insurance that provide security. The tensions to which you point are inevitable so long as we are forced to operate within the limits set by the market system. This is why it is important to be more assertive in contesting the logic of the capitalist economy itself. We need to take on the structural features of economic life that are the underlying obstacles to the introduction of policy that would allow us to approach the question of work and free time in more constructive ways.

Again one can see a similar tension over the government's proposed pit closures. On the one hand coal causes acid rain and the trucks that transport it create pollution so there is obviously the need for a more rational energy policy yet the whole country has rallied around the cause of the miners and the popular mood is that they have a right to work. How do we square the need for a sound energy policy while still supporting the miners' rights to jobs?

It is possible to think of energy conservation projects as well as energy exploitation. The pit closures have brought home the irrationality of a policy that deals with scarce resources by throwing them into competition, and finds the gas board praying for a cold winter in order to sustain its profitability. It has also exposed the hypocrisy of speaking of market forces as if they were some indomitable natural dynamic which has the nasty side-effects of throwing people on the dole and destroying communities, but to which we must none the less inevitably accommodate. The pit closure decision has alerted us to the ways in which these forces are in fact subject to political manipulation, and shown up the curious Alice in Wonderland logic which allows the Tories to defend pit closures to make sure coal will not be economic in future. But in the end, the problem has to do with the globalisation of capital, which sets the context within which national economies react to these kinds of crises.

So the response should be couched in terms which look beyond the constraints imposed by the global market and seek to break with them. Rather than talking exclusively in terms of the 'right to work', we should be questioning the methods of production which allow no alternative between the dole queue on the one hand or a life time of hard – and often health impairing – labour on the other. Equally, we should be contesting the pit closures not simply in terms of the viability of coal over other sources of energy, or the way coal is going to be crucial to meeting expanding energy needs but within the framework of an alternative policy whose primary focus is on conservation and a healthier and cleaner environment.

What would a rational energy programme be?

A responsible energy policy should scrap nuclear power and look for ways of restraining energy use. This means rethinking the question of lifestyle along lines which allow for a sustainable level of energy consumption. Developing alternative energy sources will have a part to play in this process but we should not hope for miracles. Again it comes back to the realism of thinking in more utopian – less resource dependent – terms about our pleasure.

As you point out, the Labour Party lacks the imagination to present any viable alternative vision. Would proportional representation (PR), which is most likely to be achieved through a Labour-Liberal realignment, create the space for the sort of party that could take up a new socialist programme? For example, the Green Party advocated many of the ideas you describe, would PR have made success more likely?

We are in a defensive position vis-a-vis the strength of free market ideas so anything that promises to shift sections of society around ideas of citizenship and democracy is important, and a realignment of Liberal and Labour thinking could be constructive in that area. PR is essential for thinking in terms of an alternative political formation in the long term. The initiatives for an eco-socialist alternative are dependent on the introduction of PR and realignment could assist this in the medium term. PR would also have been very helpful in introducing more ethical policies, such as those advocated by the Green Party, into party politics.

We have a two party system which is essentially 'means contesting' rather than 'ends questioning'. Party differences are about how best to realise an agreed set of aims – improved living standards, making Britain more competitive, and so on – rather than about the nature and desirability of the goals themselves. This cross party consensus has blocked the political imagination around other realisable goals. PR would have given the Green Party a higher profile and created a more favourable climate for getting its ideas across. However some of the Green Party's problems have been due to a lack of radicalism in its thinking about the environment. If other parties were not to steal its clothes, it needed to be associated with a more forceful attack on the economic obstacles standing in the way of ecological good practice. The decline of support for the Green Party and its consequent internal troubles are partly due to the 'greening' of the other parties, however opportunistic and cosmetic their commitments at this level may be.

However, people are disillusioned with party politics and feel distanced from political machinery. So is it not the realignments at local levels, where individuals through collectives are reflecting a new radical citizenship and their own autonomy and interests while respecting other people's rights and needs, that the real initiatives are emerging?

Yes, it is encouraging that people are seizing grass roots initiatives. They are doing this because party politics does not articulate forms of opposition and dissatisfaction which are felt around issues of identity and local needs. So there has been a shift to a more specifically targeted and locally based type of politics. Social movements have also begun to function as a sort of alternative welfare provision which compensates for the erosion of state provided services. In the long term this can be helpful in politicising people and restoring a sense of responsibility and power over their communities. But it is difficult to see how the various strands can come together in some integrated and radical democratic alterna-

tive without the synthesising force of a party or institutional representation. That is why pluralism is not in itself a solution – in
many ways it is the name of a problem. How do you pull all these
different demands together and end up only with the good and
none of the abrasions?

**But surely we need a politics that goes beyond the institutional-
ist and statist context of a party if we are really serious about
empowering people to take charge of their own lives? Do we not
want a radical diffusion of power away from political parties?**

There is a need to diffuse power and to allow people to voice their
own needs. The political education and empowerment that comes
from engaging in local campaigns and taking the initiative is politically important. But it is also important to distinguish the
demand for diffusion and decentralisation, which is part of the left
conception of personal empowerment, from Tory ideology which
is eroding welfare services and deploring state intervention in the
name of individual responsibility and participation. We need to
develop democratic structures which free people from a bureaucratic and paternalistic welfare provision without leaving them to
cope with life, or the care of others such as the elderly and handi-
capped, entirely on the basis of their private resources. To place
emphasis solely on empowerment is to come close to some of the
Tory arguments used to justify continued cuts in public spending.
Decentralisation, moreover, does not provide for the forms of economic management which are ecologically needed. These will
arguably require more centralised organisation.

**But a centralised state structure responsible for managing the
economy would necessarily have to infringe on the minutiae of
individual rights which are considered sacrosanct.**

There would be restraints on individual freedom. But this is why
democracy is so important. People must ask to have these constraints placed on them by a party through a popular mandate.
Respect for democracy makes it crucial that people vote within a
multi-party system for the forms of policing to which they wish to
be subjected, for example in their use of resources.

**So without any effective party structure that can articulate an
alternative socialist vision the hopes of a socialist revival do not**

seem very promising. Is the future outlook more optimistic?

It will be a very long haul. At present there is a firm, if minority, commitment to left-wing specific issue campaigns and some signs of a resurgence of a more class-based politics around the pit closures. If you could put those two together you have the beginnings of a promising articulation of class and social movements. This coupled with the benefits of possible democratisation of a Liberal-Labour realignment could be helpful in changing the political climate. But there is not going to be a quick solution. We are talking about forms of change which depend on many different stimuli and will only come about, if they do, in a very gradual way.

Hite Strikes Back

Shere Hite interviewed by **Denise Searle**

SHERE HITE BECAME involved in the women's movement in the early 1970s by joining a picket of typewriter manufacturer Olivetti over a sexist advertising campaign. The advertisement, showing two dishevelled models, was captioned: 'The typewriter that's so smart that she doesn't have to be'. Hite was one of the 'dumb' models. Despite this unorthodox introduction to women's issues, within six years Hite had become one of the best known feminist figures on both sides of the Atlantic. Her 1976 *Hite Report on Female Sexuality* was the first work to document women's views of sex. The report, based on 3,000 anonymous questionnaire responses in the US, shocked the male establishment by saying what women knew all along – that most women masturbate and most women orgasm more easily through clitoral stimulation than sexual intercourse. The report challenged many other sexual stereotypes and, in the feminist climate of the 1970s, was warmly received.

Her next two works hit rockier ground. The 1981 *Hite Report on Male Sexuality and Masculinity* showed widespread ignorance among US men about sex and women's sexuality and led to Hite being branded a 'man hater'. Worse was to come in 1987 with *Women and Love: A Cultural Revolution in Progress*, which presented questionnaire replies from 4,500 women and showed many to be in despair over the emotional quality of their close relationships with men. This time it was not only the tabloid press which attacked Hite; some British feminists such as Lynne Segal joined in attacking her methodology, accusing her of 'picking and choosing from millions of quotes to say what she wants'. They complained about the lack of class analysis and the 'romantic individualism' of

US feminists. 'It's this soft radical feminism,' says Segal, 'it reckons women's values are always good and capable of changing the world.' Despite the battering, Hite is now back with a new book, *Women as Revolutionary Agents of Change 1972-93* (London: Bloomsbury, 1993), a collection of the abstract writings that were not published with the previous works, plus defences of her scientific methods. The book is intended to be a groundwork for Hite's study of the family, due out next year. 'Soft' is not an adjective that springs to mind after a conversation with Hite. She does believe women's cooperative ideals could change society for the better, but advocates more militancy in exerting them.

Denise Searle: The women's movement in the US seems very much alive at the moment. The threat to abortion rights seems to have galvanised a wide range of feminists, while younger women are also coming up with their own ideas.

Shere Hite: Yes, the women's movement became very active around the issues of Anita Hill and sexual harassment, abortion rights, and getting Bill Clinton elected, although the Democrats tend to take women's votes for granted, like they used to take black votes. But at least Clinton's presidency should help stop the violence against women that was clandestinely promoted by the Bush and Reagan administrations. I think the women's movement is in for another 10 year active period. Some of the backlash against women in the US seems to be over. There seems to be a new moment.

The term 'backlash' is a misnomer because it implies that we pushed too far and that there is a swing back against us. But we never pushed that far, we never got our own way.

This is a very profound point. But some people, especially fundamentalists of all religions, got very frightened of the progress that feminism was making, at least in terms of rhetoric, and this has caused some of the reactionary counter attack – almost an attempted counter reformation, an end to the separation of church and state.

You also make the point in your books that many men still don't see women's liberation as liberating them too. And when you step outside the left where many men have taken on board at

least some principles of equality, it's frightening to see how engrained chauvinism still is.

Now there is a clear understanding that it is unacceptable to discriminate against blacks in the US. Most people would be afraid to be openly racist. However, with feminism, consciousness has not yet gotten even that far, although hopefully we can arrive at that stage at some point. But this could be more difficult because inequality reaches into the home and is even more fundamental. It is the basis of patriarchy: what reward do they give men for being loyal to the system? They give them women to be their own possessions at home. I wish men would say outright why they cannot accept equality; I wish they would look more deeply into themselves and ask why.

I have just re-read the first *Hite Report* [into women's sexuality] and I was amazed at how little has changed. How do you feel when you look back at that original work?

I feel pretty good. The basic idea holds, that 'sex' as we know it is a cultural not a biological institution, and that there is a terrible oppression of women in the way it is defined. There was a period when the idea of clitoral stimulation at least, if not the undefining of sex [allowing many definitions of sex other than just intercourse] was accepted. But among many younger women these ideas are disappearing into the woodwork under the deluge of cultural stereotypes, so it's a good time to repeat this analysis.

Do you think women are any more in control of our sexuality than we were 20 years ago? I'm thinking of the Madonna phenomenon where she gives the impression of women being in control, but is actually pandering to men's fantasies.

She seems to feel so little conflict about presenting stereotypes which please men. Maybe she feels that by holding a mirror to society she causes some men to think. But friends in Germany say: 'No, she just causes them to jerk off.' But then art seems to have special privileges over politics, artists are often held up as rebels when their 'message' is really just reinforcing the system.

Originally women identified with Madonna; they felt her sexy image was as much for herself as for men. But now she seems to have crossed a divide and the people who identify with her are men.

What is particularly worrying is that men say Madonna illustrates the point that women are more sexually liberated than they used to be. A supposed example of this is the prevalence of explicit articles on sex used to sell up-market women's magazines. These articles may be dressed up in a slightly more salacious way, but the bottom line is 'How to please your man'. We are living under a dangerous misconception because men say we are stronger and getting our own way whereas the same old stereotypes are being reinforced.

The image of Madonna gives the impression that women can be as sexual as they like (without being stigmatised) but that is not true. People watch Madonna as they watched Marilyn Monroe. It's like a morality play: 'Woman defies stereotypes, woman will die' is the scenario they believe usually happens. If Madonna lives to be 90, proving them wrong, it might change something. The part of me that likes Madonna worries about her.

You mean she is not really as in control as she appears to be, that she is being manipulated by the system?

I hope that the system does not kill her. Maybe the danger is a kind of ideological death. Earlier on she seemed to be her own person. She wants to go towards films and is not finding this easy. It is hard for women to get ahead in the rock business, so you have to admire her for that.

You and your books have come in for a lot of criticism in the past, would you with hindsight have handled things differently?

The criticisms would have happened anyway. Maybe someone else would have had another manner, but if you try to say something more politely it's not heard. I try to make the things I say as straightforward as possible. There certainly was a furore and it got worse with each book. I got more facts through the media initially, but with every subsequent book I could get less through. This tendency was increased by the climate in the US during the 1980s. By 1981 when I published the second book, Ronald Reagan was in office and he had arrived screaming: 'The press is too left.' There was also a concentration of media ownership and all this combined to give an unbalanced view.

How do you feel when you get criticism closer to home? Some feminists, while welcoming the books, have criticised the

methodology, for example the lack of random surveys.

It is not people who have read my books who wonder about my scientific method. There are many scientific methods; there is no one universal method. Few people do random samples any more. They call them random but they are not. Marketing research tries to use random samples, but people refuse to answer, and if you don't get 70 per cent of the people you have picked randomly answering, your sample is blotto. So they fill in the other 30 per cent. That explains why so many election samples are inaccurate, for example in the last election here.

Another criticism is that the research doesn't reach working class people, that the length of the questionnaires used to evaluate people's feelings about sex and relationships and the sophistication of the questions means that replies will tend to come from the articulate, sexually aware, highly educated middle class.

This is not true. The answers came from all kinds of women. What was shocking was that the work revealed the feminisation of poverty in the US. I was shocked at the number of single women with children who wrote that their income was $5,000 (£3,400) a year. A lot of those were educated as middle class women. Does that mean, that because you are a single parent and you have almost no income that you are working class? Or since you are educated that makes you middle class? The categories are becoming increasingly blurred. There need to be new categories, or more categories. If a woman is married to a middle class white man and he has an income of x, y or z, and she is a housewife, she is sharing the income but it is not hers. Is she poor? I would say so.

Your writings pay attention to the idea of economic independence.

In the first book too, I wrote a chapter called Sexual Slavery, which asked, 'Is it possible to know if you want to have intercourse with somebody or if you are really in love with them if you are financially dependent?' My books are presented more as a debate between women – they are not trying to tell somebody else how to be.

Is your work sociology, psychology or cultural analysis?

There is such a confusion about my work in the minds of many people. For example if you want to know how many women have orgasms during intercourse, you need to do a statistical survey. Nobody else, before or after, except women's magazines, have asked that question. But who knows if you ever are perfectly statistically representative? I said 70per cent of women do not have orgasms during intercourse. I do not know whether this is precise for women all over the globe but it does seem to apply to the majority of women. Otherwise they have had 15 years to say this is not the case and that has not happened. The physical questions require one kind of research and presentation, but when you are asking how is it going in your relationship this requires a different approach. What women say about love is often presented as a debate.

Maybe the debating aspect is what draws criticism, especially from parts of the left in Britain who like to deal with absolutes. They have read their political theory and want clear answers. They can be a very harsh audience. Your books often raise more questions than you answer and they are uncomfortable with that.

Yes, many people were frustrated with the last book. In interviews after *Women and Love* the first question would be: 'Well, how do we make the revolution?' People would like to make the next step, but if we are trying not to be authoritarian or dogmatic and not to have only one system, how do we move forward? We are in a process of debate about the system we would like to build.

The days of a strict agenda are gone?

Yes, how can we have a debate otherwise? The problem with the older communist movement in the US was its 'You have to shut up and salute the leader' attitude.

And often they would say to women: 'Be patient sister, come the revolution you will have emancipation.'

That is what they say to Black women now. In the US, Black women are more likely to have jobs than their husbands. But they are told, because they're working, they should shut up and support their man as he's already got enough problems.

Your next book is on the family?

I've finished research on one aspect of the family, the power of parents over their children. According to official statistics only 7 per cent of the British population are in the nuclear family of 2.2 children. So why is the nuclear family mythology still so pervasive? Part of the reason for my doing the book is the fundamentalist attack on women's rights, as symbolised by abortion rights in Europe and the US. The credo is that women have to be mothers, so a witch hunt goes on if a woman wants an abortion – since this must mean that she does not want to be a mother. And films like *Fatal Attraction* and *Single White Female* portray women who do not fit the creche stereotype as monsters. If the stereotypes remain in place about who women should be – and many of them come from the family system which came from the church reinforced by the state – how do you change those? Do you just supplant them by others? Do you just say these are rotten stereotypes, we need to have new stereotypes? It's the difficulty of holding a debate. Can you get people to go with you when you don't know exactly where you're going? Maybe that's one of the stumbling blocks for men. In terms of restructuring their relationships with women, even in the workplace, since they don't know what the outcome should be, maybe this inhibits them from trying.

You have mentioned that women are still marginalised. What do you see as the way forward? How do we start trying to win a better position or equality?

The main problem for women is the taboo on anger, on being angry with men, that is, the social order in which men rule. Yet if men are the main group that has power over us we have to be angry with that group; but to be angry with that group defines you as 'unfeminine', according to the stereotype. It is circular. Young feminists ask why older feminists do not help them more. We thought we were helping; we bashed our heads against a brick wall trying to get our message across, yet the media frequently distorted what we did. The media message sometimes is: 'If you're a young groovy hip woman you don't have to be angry like those older women. It'll be fine because you are the new generation! Of course "those older women" are bitter because they had those struggles.' Ironically, younger women have gotten the message with every new generation since the 1920s. The 'good woman' is a happy woman; the benign mother stereotype is perpetuated – 'Just smile and shuffle.' But we are never going to get equality by smiling and shuffling. We did not get the vote that way, and we will not get anything else that way either. It's going to have to be taken.

When a woman is strong we're often accused of being like a man, but men are not necessarily strong. They are often competitive or aggressive, but when a woman is strong or even ruthless it does not necessarily mean we are aping male behaviour.

I agree. Anger often comes out in a dogmatic way in the beginning, but that is okay, it has to come out some way.

We need to get away from this tyranny, almost, in some women's circles of...

...being nice. The tyranny of 'to be nice'.

Yes, and that can be damaging, this stereotype that sisterhood means everybody hugging and listening.

That is an important point, this thing that we have to be nice, or 'motherly' – you can't be angry if you are a woman or use that anger as a direction to go in, especially against men. It would be interesting to see the direction for action our debate leads us to in the next few years, if we put aside those stereotypes.

OPENING UP OUR VISION

Stuart Hall interviewed by Adam Lent

Adam Lent: Perhaps I could begin by raising the issue of the need for the left to have a general vision of society. Do you feel that the basis for an intellectual-political renewal, rather than an immediate organisationa – political renewal, is being built through the ideas that are now flowing from Green ideals and principles of radical democracy? Or might they come from other sources?

Stuart Hall: There are many areas in which useful thinking is going on. Even the disaster of the 1992 Rio summit gave a kick to ecological consciousness. Questions of constitutional reform were around during the election, albeit in a truncated form. There are plenty of ideas but what I feel is lacking at the moment is the climate in which those ideas become articulated to political projects. Part of the problem is that the Labour Party undertakes its thinking with a very restricted access. They have a kind of tame intellectual elite but they do not have any connection to, and are deeply suspicious of, any wider intellectual currents. This is astonishing given the fact that not only academia but all intellectuals in Britain tend to have to make their living through teaching, and that education has been so badly treated by the right. Additionally many of these intellectuals are absolutely dying for somebody to talk to them but nobody does. And in some areas there are not many ideas around – on the central question of what is the nature of 'the public' under conditions where socialism and radical reform are not going to be administered by a unified and coherent state power; how does the state relate to a much more diverse range of publics? It cannot be understood in terms of just five-yearly elections or opinion polls. And the critical question about how we escape from the old bureaucratic, clientist forms while avoiding the Thatcherite model is not being addressed either. There is a lot of thinking and ideas coming from those working in the public sector that are not tied to the old centralised bureaucracies. They are talking to each other but they are not part of a wider debate.

But there is a wide range of activities underway. There are campaigns for centre-left realignment, for constitutional reform and there is a plethora of social movements which are still active despite the attacks of the last 13 years. So how can those movements begin to come together? Should they be trying to get together?

There are different strategies. One is to work out if there is some type of organisational form which might create better contact across different groups, but without electoral reform that formation could be cut to ribbons. You have to think very carefully about how we might insert such a formation into the two-party system, both because there are constituencies out there that need change now and cannot wait till the next decade and because a fifth Conservative term will finish us all off.

The more important concern is the Labour Party and its instrumentality and connection with a range of movements and ideas in civil society – they do not need formal organisational linkage but a radial point into the thinking and strategy of the party. There are two ways to go. One is a kind of semi-autonomous, quasi-party organisation made up of those elements that are left out of the particular political configuration. This raises the question of how does that bring itself to bear on the actual electoral mobilisation, voting and tasks of forming a government. On the other hand can we change the Labour Party so that it acts not as the agent of its own rather sclerotic thinking, but as the conduit for a much wider set of ideas, movements, agitations and experiences? It is unclear which option might be more successful. In some ways it might be easier for those groups to talk to one another because they have many political and cultural things in common. But that means you just leave the Labour Party to wither on the vine, which would have very serious consequences for the balance of political forces.

What then are the political and cultural things that these various progressive forces have in common? Some attempts at networks,

for example the Socialist Movement, have not been eminently successful. Attempts to bring together different groups only seems to highlight their differences.

The common factors are not there simply to be discovered. After all, these groups are the consequence of a fragmentation of the political landscape which does not easily cohere into an overall vision of a future social direction. That is definitely one problem. Another is that simply by networking the social movements and other currents as they stand is not sufficient to bring them up against the actual trend and direction of society. That is the disciplining factor. All these things must have a purchase on a society which is not currently giving ecological questions the kind of priority they want and which is still very deeply committed to an individualist path to success. Unless you do come into sharp conflict with these factors, the movements and currents are working in a slightly protected vacuum. They are talking to one another but they have to think about the world out there in which they are going to have to mobilise if they are going to have an impact on the majority.

And do you think that it is ideas around democracy and pluralism and citizenship that could bring these groups into coalition and begin to have an impact on the society they are trying to change?

Those are critical questions. The language of rights is the only currently available one that has a lot of popular purchase and depth in which to articulate the needs of individuals and collectives. There are problems with the language of citizenship because it is very individualised – it does not assimilate easily to collective needs and collective demands. A second issue is that needs themselves are very diversified. Society has been pluralised by different experiences, aims and social worlds and the language of citizenship is pretty universal in its origins and its characteristic forms. To reflect a diversity of needs through a universalist language means there must be some negotiation which the groups involved in citizenship have not fully taken on. For example, how do you express the needs of women which are very specific within the language of universal claims? So the language of universal citizenship must include enclaves of particular claims by groups with very specific needs. There is a tension between the universal rights that citizenship delivers to all, regardless of race, gender etc, and the differentiated specificity of the needs which different groups have.

The overall political question is exactly how to integrate those different specific needs within some common political project. How to link the aspirations of the rising social strata, who still see their fortunes linked to the breakaway of the private sector and privatisation, with the completely differentiated needs of a very large underclass who cannot command an electoral majority? The rising strata may not be paid-up Thatcherites, but they can see that the good things that have happened to them in recent years have somehow been brought about by the break-up of the social democratic landscape. Citizenship might be able to provide some rights to the underclass but you have to appeal to those other social strata who might not be convinced that they will get anything good out of it.

You have described Majorism as 'unhegemonic'. Do you therefore think that it will now be easier for progressive forces to make headway against the Conservatives? Maybe the election result has made you revise your view that Majorism is in fact 'unhegemonic'?

Yes, I have changed my mind slightly. The figure of Major as a political device was rather successful in stitching together a movement towards a more altruistic, less abrasive view than Thatcherism, with a little more attention to the social fabric and to the people who have been left out, without actually making people pay the cost. It is rather well staged: he is much nicer, and obviously not wanting to grind the faces of the poor in the dust but he is not going to put a price on it either. So although it was rather successful it remains unsure whether or not it is hegemonic. And while Majorism has no distinctive project it is still deeply attached to the Thatcherite project. This means the reconstruction of the institutional life of society, which is still rolling along. Major gives his own gloss to that which makes it slightly more acceptable to public opinion but it has not halted that underlying drift. And people have not latched on to this. There is rather more momentum in the Thatcherite project than we imagined.

In the echelons of liberal opinion the usual British pragmatism seems to be emerging and this will adapt quietly and eventually to practically anything. If the government were to say, 'Let us murder half the population because we have to deal with the population problem', of course there would be outrage. But six months later, the liberal echelons would say, 'Well, we cannot do anything about it, it has been legislated for; we should be thinking about how we can do it humanely.' The *Guardian* ran four articles saying that it was ridiculous to publish the league tables of schools but, since we have to, we will find the best way of doing it. That kind of pragmatic adaptation to anything that is put forward is very well established.

In a sense we are still on the rolling tide of the Thatcherisation of society and Major is still attached to that underlying project. However, Major's project does not have quite the glamour of success around it as compared with the early 1980s. And the wobble in the economy will produce counter-ideas as well as other sources of resistance. If the Tories were transforming society and delivering on the economic front, it would be very hard to see any openings. The weakness of the economy just opens the gap within which other doubts can be seeded. So resistance will not go away but it is unlikely that Majorism will break-up from inside.

But what is terrifying is that Thatcherism and the Conservative Party has this incredible ability to maintain the kernel of faith in market forces while still absorbing, and adapting itself to, the accusations of its opposition. For example, on the Green issue Major has adapted himself towards an emphasis on consumer protection and the public interest. So, even if that anger that you identify does come through, will the groundswell ever be strong enough to overwhelm the Tories or will they once again be able to adapt to survive?

You are absolutely right, but it is impossible to answer in the abstract. We have underestimated the elan with which a party can be unscrupulous about opportunism and principles. Nevertheless many of the doubts we have identified are diametrically opposed to Tory philosophy, and they are sitting on top of a society without commanding even a normal electoral, popular majority. And they are aware of the fact that in order to remain in a hegemonic position they must constantly adapt, absorb, translate and transform. They are constantly buying in from society, whether it is ecology or consumer needs, and transforming ideas into their own language, by a bit of lying and bit of deception. We cannot say if they will always be able to do that until the question is asked: is the left doing the same thing? And it is not. The left is not attentive to all sorts of ideas, movements, antagonisms and needs being formulated out there in society, which it has to bring into its own orbit, to transform into a wider programme and to begin to shape legislation. The left does not function in relation to society in the same way. If it did there would be two political forces that are trying to reflect civil society within the framework of their own legislative and political philosophies.

You said that a fifth Conservative term would finish us all off, so the inevitable question, asked in semi-desperation, is what can we do to prevent that fifth term? You seem to place some of your faith in the economy but obviously there is very little that progressive forces can do now to affect that.

Many local things can be done. Alternative visions do not arise only from committees. For example, if we put some resources into a campaign to stop the destruction of our education system. We could not do it simply around defence of the old comprehensive system; we would have to ask, 'How could we construct an education system that would actually work effectively for the disenfranchised majority and create an educated public?' A lot of parents, including the so-called privatised, well-off middle class sector, still have kids in the public education system and they would respond to such a discussion. Neither the Labour Party or teachers' unions are sufficiently attentive to the genuine fears that different sections of society, such as women, blacks and middle-class parents have about the unsuccessful delivery of education as a mass public service. There is a huge range of people who would get involved in a debate on public education. Such a debate might oblige Labour and the unions to put some of their resources and political power into connecting with this public discussion and agitation.

You are suggesting that the left switch away from the defensive role it has been playing for so long now. That brings us back to the question of vision because vision is central to any hegemonic project and the objective of creating people's identities.

Absolutely. I am not opposed to the defensive role. Anyone who works in the public sector will know that half your day is going to be spent defending the base, so that there is something from which to build. But being locked into the defensive conception has been the ruin of the so-called attempts to renew the left.

It is a project that has started 10 years too late, it should have started in 1983.

Yes. When we have called for rethinking on the left, it was not for a cosmetic dropping of the parts that the polls tell us are not going down too well in Basildon. The idea was to free the ideals from the forms – the existing forms were not generating and delivering the ideals. If you think that education should be much more widely accessible as a critical resource of post-industrial society, you should not fight to the death to defend the particular forms in which that ideal was institutionalised in the 1950s. Open yourself, on the basis of that ideal, to the critique of the old form and then **ask** yourself what strategies are there for re-embodying those ideals in forms which meet the more differentiated structure of the population and the new needs of knowledge and so on. That is the only way to construct a vision.